The Sacred Revealed

POEMS TO INSPIRE AND DELIGHT

Joe Anthony

INDIA · SINGAPORE · MALAYSIA

ISBN 979-8-89133-960-6

DEDICATED TO

MY CHILDREN AND GRANDCHILDREN

CLIFTON, IRENE, SONIA

ETHAN, ERIK, NATHAN

Pondering on the Cover Design

God is the light of life and life of life. No genre of literature can define the beauty of His creation as poetry can. The inner lamp of reawakening is like an endless quest, the form of which changes as we move ahead in life, just like a river. May the light of lights lead you on the path called life.

THE SACRED REVEALED

By JOE ANTHONY

(Poems to inspire and delight)

SYNOPSIS

Poetry is both mystical and mysterious. Through this book, the author intends to take the readers to a journey of pleasure and pain, awe and wonder, which in turn would lead them through the hills and valleys of life. This book is an extension of Volume one titled A QUEST FOR THE SACRED which specifically aimed at arousing our yearning for the spiritual and spurring us to ascend heights beyond the mundane. In volume 2, titled THE SACRED REVEALED, the author leads the reader to the realization of eternal truths revealed more implicitly than explicitly by considering certain facets of life which have deep connotations but are generally overlooked or missed out on.

Arise, then, make this pilgrimage and enter the realm of the spirit. Be immersed in the essence of the unknown made known, that your insatiable desire to discover the mystery and meaning of what had been veiled is now revealed. By accepting this truth you enter into a mystical union with the Supreme Poet, the Almighty, the Source of all knowledge and wisdom, whose essence provides us with the true meaning of things.

This volume contains ten chapters, each dealing with different topics of a particular nature. This segregation may appear artificial and unsatisfactory but there is no way we can place them into water-tight compartments, because some form of overlapping is bound to emerge.

I wish you all a happy and inspiring experience.

Joe Anthony

Contents

The Sacred Revealed

I

ETERNAL TRUTHS

Certain qualities are inherent in man, others are painstakingly cultivated. They are the bedrock on which lives are based. Things inconspicuous and insignificant stare at us at all times and being so ordinary we ignore or discard them. Unfortunately, we forget, that often they teach us important truths more effectively than those we wonder at and hold in awe. To live a full and satisfying life we need to accept these compelling factors to influence us.

1. Shine Through the Dark

When things are engulfed in darkness around
Your search for a light that can't be found,
Look deep within and explore your heart
You could as well be the needed light.

The denser the darkness appears as background
The brighter the beams of light will rebound,
Immense will be the delight we gain
When relieved of extreme pangs of pain.

When you realize your life's in darkness
Fear not to flash a ray of brightness,
If problems you face offer no solutions
Burst the bubble that projects illusions.

People have succeeded in breaking free
Of darkness, failures and negativity,
If wrapped with the veil of doubt and fear
Rip it asunder and diffuse some cheer.

Problems can never defeat the daring
For they disappear when there is sharing
Fight the bleakness dormant in you
Let it fall under the sun's purview.

Convert all failures to stepping stones
Like life returning to the valley of bones
In thick darkness stars glimmer brighter
So in defeat you'll emerge a victor.

Joe Anthony

2. Super Performance

When you do your work with excellence
Let your signature have its presence,
Sign it with your ethos in effect
Let your work its perfection reflect.

Not only engage in jobs you prefer
But show love for what you defer,
Your superior nature will certainly outshine
Your work will turn out super fine.

Hard work, sincerity and devotion
Have been the hallmark of your vision
Success will embrace your dedication
Prosperity, the reward of your decision.

Don't lean on others, you'll be a weight,
Be a wall they can lean against,
Become a shady tree, look not for shade,
Light a candle, prevent darkness invade.

When the final whistle of life is blown
And time for you the world to disown,
You will bid your final goodbye
And let your triumphs God glorify.

Joe Anthony

3. Pain is a Person

I whispered softly to pain
He is a genuine person,
I can't find him in books,
But surely in people's looks.

Pain has a face of his own
By which he can be known,
His name bears a label,
A name unique and noble.

His heart pulsates with passion,
He needs love and devotion,
He's lodged in everyone's heart,
Of the public, an integral part.

Pain is present in every cheer,
Not only in loneliness and fear,
In his smile there is sadness,
But he's a stranger to gladness.

His words are full of emotion
Never give up is his slogan,
His language is truly universal
For him grief isn't eternal.

We can never part with pain
So to embrace him is a gain,
Despite all forms of strain
Forever friends we'll remain.

Joe Anthony

4. Life is a Melody

The song of life is unique and precious
Lilting with rhythm and perfect in rhyme,
Transcends the mundane and is vivacious,
Echoes a melodious voice that's sublime.

Gift-wrapped for us in time and space
This dulcet sound in awe we recall,
Unravel its mystery and warmly embrace
Expose it and offer the world to enthrall.

With a sense of depth and pellucid vision,
To beguile a world that's fully submerged
In contempt and abject dissipation,
To be the inner eye to have it purged.

This song will unfold sights of wonder
Inspire and excite a genuine yearning,
Satiate the ever growing hunger,
And subdue matters emerge alarming.

This worthy song embodies the lifebelt,
Fasten securely, be completely unnerved,
Prepare earnestly for an inner reset
And celebrate the life you anxiously craved.

Joe Anthony

5. To Live is to Struggle

Life is a struggle for most
A live or die encounter,
Along the shingled coast
On a rudderless boat in winter.

The tussle never abates or ends
In ferocity or in dimension,
Often it grows in proportions
Creating bitter dissension.

May appear gentle and silent
Like a dormant emotion,
Or very often violent
And reveals by explosion.

The battle may be of the mind
Where the stress is severe,
Or physical and harsh in kind
That affects every sphere.

They vary in form and time
Never the same all day,
Vigilance is the need prime
To counter its deadly slay.

Often you are the victim
You may not be aware,
Others too fall in the system,
Though that often seems rare.

You may struggle for the better
To create a new world order,
Or destroy an existing matter
And create a new border.

But struggle certainly you must
In times both bad and good,
The only choice is to adjust
And proceed with the right attitude.

Joe Anthony

6. In Life and in Death

At loss of wealth we worry and deliberate
But for a year's loss with cake we celebrate,
Birth announces nine months in advance
But death appears suddenly and in silence.

The reward for wealth in life we amassed
Six feet of raw soil is all that's announced,
Everything that seems pretty and appealing
Will eventually turn out worthless and fleeting.

Morning doesn't ever stretch up to noon
Nor does noon, till the arrival of the moon,
As days are buried in the grave of night
All our ventures end in death's might.

When legs grow weak and speed declines
The body rejects what the mind assigns,
Like lying on a sick bed staring at strangers
Aware of emotions averse to face dangers.

From dust were we formed, to dust we return,
The soil we walk on will cover us in turn,
God will burst open the prison of our body
Our soul will ascend to eternal glory.

Joe Anthony

7. Creation is God's Poetry

Poetry is the language of the muses,
It is sublime in form and essence
And resides in celestial ambience,
Blithesome is the feeling it diffuses.

Poetic whispers tickle the mind,
Felt only in the silence of the heart,
Excite passion to reveal the secret
And relish an inner joy refined.

Hymns are written in poetic grace
Pure and simple to affect reflection,
Befitting are such songs of devotion
In poetic cadence offered in praise.

Of all the modes of expressing feelings
None seems more effective as a poem,
Because its status is celestial and solemn
It inspires us to be clean in our dealings.

Creation is heaven's poetic rendering
Rhyme and rhythm are in reason's purview
In poetic bliss our encounters review
In ecstatic fusion our poems we sing.

Joe Anthony

8. He Spreads the Universe

God is majestic, august and immense
Vaster even than his mighty universe,
It isn't static, its essence is certain,
He spreads the universe like a curtain.

His creation echoes in awesome wonder,
His voice rips the heavens asunder,
His majesty and power him magnify,
And send his lightning to zigzag the sky.

Hear the daunting roar of his thunder,
The horrid tsunamis pillage and plunder,
He rattles the earth in violent fury,
His whirlwind swirls the clouds unruly.

Trillions of galaxies and milky ways
Deck the universe to sing out his praise,
King of all creation, the One Supreme,
Embellishes the earth with beauty extreme.

Diverse the glorious colors and designs,
Mesmerizing tapestry of wisdom and signs,
Aromatic fragrance enhancing vibrancy,
He embalms the world to assert his primacy.

Man is the ultimate symbol of his glory
Far beyond even every spiritual entity,
Thus the Almighty reveals his splendor,
Unveils his radiant and amazing grandeur.

Joe Anthony

9. Water and Wind

Wind and water are soul playmates
They frolic together on rippling waves
Wind is the player and water, the ground,
Always on the move, never get downed.

Water does a waltz in slow motion
Doesn't stay long in isolation,
Tends to be led by the ebb and flow,
Unsteady on the surface and below.

As I watch its blithesome spree
In anxious urge to reach the sea,
I too seem to swim to my end
With wind and water forever blend.

Like the wind that blows to its terminus
In time and rhythm forever unanimous
Concealed from our rational brain
Its origin or goal we can't ascertain.

Joe Anthony

10. They Are Inevitable

Pain and sorrow, my intimate friends,
Miss them whenever they're absent,
Inseparable like beginnings and ends
When they approach without my consent
I scream and denounce until they leave,
Then I find I'm left alone to grieve.

Pain is an essential part of life
An inevitable requisite to keep balance
Lest you sink when confronting strife,
Pain is a teacher par excellence,
Brings huge rewards, often unsought,
And unexpected dividends by default.

Share your suffering with that of the Lord,
Redemptive suffering is grace's bedrock
Where divine merit is your soul's reward,
A recompense so great, you'll be in shock,
And satisfaction and comfort in abundance
Inundating you in the flood of grace.

In the crucible of suffering you're purified
As smoldering embers keep on flickering
Your sufferings are accepted and glorified,
You're bestowed with a privileged blessing.
Sufferings accepted in grateful embrace
Draw God's attention your sins to erase.

Joe Anthony

11. Sacraments Heal

Why put sacraments to the farthest side
It's the most important factor to preside
Over our disordered and paralyzed being,
Like rays that penetrate us with healing.

The bleeding woman felt only his garment
To touch his body wasn't her intent,
Healing went out through his clothing
That's how sacraments graces bring.

Approach Jesus the eternal doctor
Show your wounds and ask for succor,
This divine physician will heal you in time
For services he won't charge you a dime.

Gradual yet startling will be the healing
Without his assistance we can do nothing,
Healing is always about communion
About restoring what's been broken.

Receive not Jesus but become he,
He demands your heart, offer it free,
When he plunges into the sea of humanity
The waves travel to the ends of eternity.

Each sacrament gives us the special dignity
Of a profound and Jesus identity,
Stepping out of grace hardens our heart
And sacraments, the needed remedy impart.

When you pull a sheet over your face
You think you're safe from harmful rays,
Let the sacraments wrap you in their efficacy
Guard and defend you from the Devil's treachery.

Joe Anthony

12. Loss of Vision

We've lost our way in our search for forage,
The effective food for the soul in drought,
Loss of vision is a devastating hemorrhage,
A tsunami of commotion in the throes of doubt.

The beacon of light that led to the truth
Is marred by a dismal and foreboding cloud,
Our vision fractured and no more astute
Is a distilled version of an uncanny shroud!

In the wilderness of emptiness and deception
Our ambition is deflected from its source,
Only a firm resolve can alter our perception
And direct us to assist the truth to enforce.

Joe Anthony

13. The Windows of the Soul

We keep the windows shut
For fear of insects and dust,
Our homes are often closed
And, in our absence, locked.

Harmful elements could enter,
Thieves to break in venture,
Watchmen posted at the gate
Any intrusion they can negate.

Why so slack and casual
For the safety of the internal?
For good enters with evil
Through the windows of the soul.

Our eyes are those entries
Screened and let in by sentries,
Our soul perceives the truth
With the keen eyes of faith.

Joe Anthony

14. The Candle is Symbolic

A flickering candle in the womb of darkness,
A symbol of the light and love of the spirit,
Radiates messages of warmth and kindness
Creates a feeling of optimism infinite.

The sparkling light has a calming effect,
Its warmth, a feeling of love inflames.
The ambiance provides a scene to reflect
And a symbol of goodness it proclaims.

We are like candles burning at the altar
Flickering and melting at the same time,
The prayers and sacrifices we offer
Will echo when the church bells chime.

A candle could glow dim or bright,
Must keep on burning until the end,
An intruder could its life disrupt,
Be alert and vigilant, our life to defend.

Joe Anthony

15. Search

Search and you shall find
Was the Lord's command,
There isn't a time limit,
Search from morning to night.

Seek within yourself,
All around and beyond,
In people of every kind,
Have their words defined.

Search in the face of people,
Delve deep into their eyes,
The result that is revealed
Had been well concealed.

Search in the heavens above
Or in the earth beneath,
In darkness and in shadow,
The result of the search will show.

Search in times of peace
And when storms increase,
In the speed of a turbulent wind
That scatters things around.

Search in the core of a flower,
In the rough bark of the timber,
Study the stem of a rosebush
Thorns can be lying in ambush.

In the withered hand a laborer
In the sweltering sweat of his brow,
See the begging bowl of a toddler,
Look into the brain of a scholar.

Search the attic off sight
There you could find the truth
And in basement hidden from view,
The truth you'd tried to pursue.

There's no dearth of place
Your answer can't surface
It depends on how you seek
In vigor or in mind weak.

Seek with all eagerness,
With love, resolve and trust,
Search with a receptive mindset
With a pliant honest reset.

Seek alone or in groups
Where the vision is one,
You can't be misled by views
Thrust on you with reviews.

Joe Anthony

16. What I Didn't Know

He watched me from a distance,
Plunging into a mortal trance
I dared not share my presence
For fear of divulging my essence.

My ethos I need to integrate
Confirming to a larger estate,
He knew what I didn't know,
Though he seemed my arch foe.

I concealed all affairs of shame
From friends and patrons of fame,
Striving to pursue the trend
Ventured to the void's end.

There some strange eyes stared
Piercing the core of my being,
I stood visually impaired,
My faculties went reeling.

Then from above a dew drop
Struck me on my bald-pate,
Balancing without any prop
I regained my unsteady gait.

It wasn't a foe who watched
He was my guardian angel,
He seemed firm and bothered
But truly he was gentle.

The transforming power of grace
With faith in him enshrined,
The track I began to retrace
And found myself redesigned.

Joe Anthony

17. A New Good Samaritan

I was passing through my fading autumn,
Saw withered leaves flapping and waving,
Their early farewell was truly awesome,
They showered me with their love and blessing.

I entered a desert of loneliness and pain,
The dust of regret blinded my eyes,
My benumbed senses I couldn't maintain
My journey was delayed due to my sighs.

I saw helplessness stare at my face
Mocking me for my delicate profile,
The cause of my estate they failed to trace
So I was declared unfit and senile.

Exposed to the mercy of varied elements
I crawled to a patch of love and trust,
I was welcomed with fine sentiments,
With deep emotion I returned robust.

Joe Anthony

18. Spiritual Freedom

Detachment results in spiritual freedom,
Parting from possessions is true wisdom,
A natural tendency, an insatiable craving,
For name and fame and wealthy living.

The rejected, unknown and the maligned
Are more worthy in heaven's mind,
Living a life hidden and ordinary
Is not what the world would agree.

Abe was an apostle of mercy and caring
For he accepted the poor and the suffering,
Found his freedom by self-effacing,
And by an austere life embracing.

Joe Anthony

19. Our Inner Eye

We see things with external eyes
Enjoy good sights and reject others,
Judge them as our minds suggest,
Accept them, if their views we attest.

Eyes can reveal a mighty bunch,
Moods and emotions of varied tinge,
Convey warmth, or tones hostile,
They are gateways to enter our soul.

There is a mystical invisible eye,
Imparts insights beyond the ordinary,
Reflects the deepest emotive shades,
Which the normal eye usually evades.

Even the physically blind from birth
Can perceive what we fail to unearth,
For the sharp sword of insight can pierce
The hidden truths veiled by mortal fears.

The third eye is a force most mystical
That conveys rules that are fundamental,
Sights and sounds are non-essential,
Its essence is spiritual and celestial.

The outer eyes can deceive our view,
And project sights we wrongly construe,
The inner eye stands steadfast and true,
The safety of our soul is its prime issue.

Joe Anthony

20. The Outcome of Joy

Smile is the fruit of content
You enjoy as life's reward,
The external portrayal is meant
To confirm this all can afford.

Smile in the gloom of distress,
In the throes of intense pain,
If emerging tears you suppress
It'll blur your vision again.

Smile in the midst of fear
You will ease the burden,
Aid every strain disappear
And wrap up the job undone.

Smile through the misty eyes,
Gaze beyond the dim patch,
Shoo the moth that flies
And blocks the scene you watch.

Smile through your racking mind,
Select an inspiring melody,
Sing it with a lark and unwind,
Your grief will find a remedy.

Smile when seething with anger
Reign in its defiant power,
Caress its mane, no danger,
It will be a lamb as ever.

Joe Anthony

21. Death of the Dying

Awaiting death is the most terrible emotion
The terminally ill ones feel by premonition,
Death is certain and it could be any time,
Be prepared for it and make it sublime.

Waiting is tormenting and unappealing,
Can't express in words their silent feeling,
The lump in their throat is a bolder large
No gasp can escape even if you enlarge.

Visiting such patients is like tied to a wheelchair
Helpless beyond anything you might dare,
Pity their agony and blend with their pains
To reduce their anxiety is all that remains.

You haven't stood up all through these years
But you know you will, when he allays your fears,
His hand will lift you and make you stand
You only need to follow his command.

Joe Anthony

22. Our Destination

Beyond the shimmering pearl-studded portal
Where streamers of light glimmer immortal,
A radiant shore with a magnificent view
Shall enthrall us with its glorious hue.

Blithesome and gay are its gardens and fields,
Fadeless its blossoms that heaven shields,
Untouched or polluted by the finger of time
But nurtured and nourished by dew sublime.

Life when ebbs and weakens our breath
We shall await the glow of death,
Reclining on this shell-girded beach
Sail in a yacht and our destination reach.

Joe Anthony

23. His Vision

God unleashed a torrent of graces,
A windblast of delightful caresses,
A tidal wave of blessings in addition
To enable us to accept his own vision.

Let every heartbeat, every pulse race,
Every breath that erupts sing his praise,
Let them be concrete claims of gratitude
Offered him in a reverential attitude.

His vision is projected into our conscience
And is revealed in his words in abundance,
Blessed indeed are we to have obtained
The means in us his vision to be retained.

Joe Anthony

24. Echo from Heaven

Their angelic voices are heard
When God in heaven is adored,
With melodious songs of praise
In endless strain they raise.

Music is heaven's ethos,
Every melody has pathos,
God's voice is music
To the ears of the public.

Singing isn't my passion
Though I love to listen,
Sweet songs stir my soul
Also enthrall and console.

Peace and serenity inspire,
To set our souls afire,
Elevate mundane desire
To nobler values aspire.

Music eases pain,
Reduces stress and strain,
Urges an uplift of spirit,
And peace and joy remit.

Memories happy or sad
Are fondly remembered,
Generates energy and zest,
Exhorts to give out our best.

Joe Anthony

25. Appearance is Deceptive

He looks harsh, cruel and bold,
Scornful, wry and ready to explode,
Often grumpy and seldom smiles,
His awful presence our ambience defiles.

We view the stranger with false perception
For our judgment is misled by deception,
Appearance affects our view of his nature,
An unfair judgment in guilt we nurture.

A person may emerge calm and serene
Or irascible and haughty in disposition,
In such cases we could be irrational
And our verdict will definitely be partial.

He could be a singer trained to entertain
Having a golden voice concealed within,
An artist who loves to sketch and paint,
An athlete of high caliber, fit to compete.

Impeccable character and gentle demeanor
One could even pose a religious preacher,
Looks can't define or penetrate through
For deceit misleads and hides what's true.

Good looking people get better jobs easily
Produces results, makes friends speedily,
It's a false presumption to success and progress,
The only yardstick is the real issue to address.

We camouflage our emotions to hide reality,
Smile at the world to show distress a fallacy,
Conceal our inner state to project the wrongs
Our face reveals what to the mind belongs.

Joe Anthony

26. Get Out of Sodom

Do not enter the land of Sodom
It is the land, a symbol of evil,
For its ruler is vile as the Devil,
You'll be a slave there without freedom.

Get out Sodom if you've entered,
Be baptized in the water of the Nile,
God will part the sea for a while
Rescue you from the land you ventured.

Sodom is a nation of idolatry,
Superstition, error and sorcery,
Effeminacy, sensuality, and immorality
Are traps to accuse and frame you guilty.

Our spiritual Sodom needs a cleansing
From plagues and pestilence need fencing,
Actions and mindsets that are perverted
Should indeed be dislodged and aborted.

We visit Sodom when we tend to indulge
In alliance unnatural and overtly divulge
And promote it earnestly as a regular trend,
Which is abnormal and it does offend.

A spiritual Sodom is hidden within us
Within individuals, families and nations,
We worship liberty in perverted posture,
We should avoid this golden calf culture.

Joe Anthony

27. My Sketch Book

It's a veritable and novel album
Comprises a curious amalgam
Of sketches and paintings combine,
It's recent and original in design.

Lines and curves of the pencil,
The light and shadows essential,
And colors that vibrate with zest,
All are visible at their best.

In lieu of these I employ
Words that enrich and bring joy,
Gentle, smooth and vibrant,
Booming, resounding or silent.

Colorful words, bright and fair,
Of wisdom to inspire and share,
To make one laugh or weep,
And soothing lullaby for sleep.

I draw words with rhythm and rhyme
In figurative ways for mood sublime
Words with wings and words that dance
And words that usher in urge to romance.

Joe Anthony

28. Our Portrait

We don't hesitate to pose for a photo-shoot
Our sparkling eyes following smiles in pursuit
The image projected reflects the original
We hate if the product to us seems abnormal.

People may put up a radiant face
As a pleasing facade to hide a disgrace,
A persistent fear, worry or tension,
A painful torment they refuse to mention.

We prefer to construe facts our own way
Far from the truth that they portray,
Mistake shadow for actual substance,
But don't penetrate its real essence.

Each shoot that peeps through narrow cracks
After a cold spell of inertia's impacts,
Relishes the warmth of morning rays
And delights when spring its odor sprays.

When life is fun it's easy to sing,
Lacking essentials will always sting,
Hearts like granite, cold in their dealings
Need to be energized to revive feelings.

We go through suffering offering prayers
Hoping for success in all our affairs,
In human story and divine mystery
We are privileged to earn this victory.

Don't stifle hope but Irrigate and nourish it.
Improving lifestyle is, for sure, in its ambit,
Hope is the food on our table to partake
For God is the Provider, he'll not forsake.

Between nature, grace, grit and glory,
Between reason and the revelation story,
God intervenes and grants us exemption,
And offers us pardon and complete redemption.

Joe Anthony

29. The Human Soul

When I had been fashioned
And in my mother's womb laid
God breathed into my nostril,
And His breath formed my soul.

His gift, the immortal spirit,
His mirror image explicit
With features he possessed,
Freely on me bestowed.
The living entity that resides
In our body and us guides
Is a valid spiritual spark
Of the Supreme being's mark.

It is consciously aware
Of this transcendent power,
It provides the vital energy
To shield the soul from its enemy.

The soul partakes of the divine
Enables us to think and reason.
Makes our nature benign,
and with God's essence align.

The soul is spiritual and immortal,
Our life's vital principle,
To kill our soul there's no power
It's ordained by the Creator.

Joe Anthony

30. Gradual Perception

On wings of wonder's environ
I soared the dizzying heights,
Surveying the azure delights
Outlining the distant horizon.

Navigating the breeze in pursuit
To reach a target defined,
With fleecy clouds aligned
I dived to a strata of repute.

Lush green fanciful meadows
Decked with gorgeous flowers
Wrapped in ecstatic powers
Offered me precious mementoes.

I skipped over snow-crowned peaks
Darted through dense foliage
Swept over arid wastage
And waded in the marshy creeks.

Saluting the master of creation
I bowed in total surrender,
On his marvels began to ponder
As I glided the final turn.

Joe Anthony

II

PAIN AND SUFFERING

Pain refers to physical discomfort and emotional distress. Pain can be a source of suffering. Suffering implies conscious endurance of pain or distress. It can make us more resilient and better able to endure hardships. Suffering turns our focus inward to discover new aspects hidden within. Seeking joy in suffering gives us purpose and makes us like Jesus. Some suffering in life cannot be avoided. What cannot be avoided has to be endured.

31. Life is An Amalgam

Into my lap fell a plentitude of grace,
In ecstatic cheer of glory and praise
I raised a hymn of gratitude in place,
And received in return divine embrace.

Fortune and success, name and fame
Are all part of a mundane game,
Serenity, peace and joy proclaim
The celestial grandeur of God's holy name.

Pain and sorrow, failure and loss,
Defeat, rejection and emptiness,
Sinful lifestyle of glamour and gloss
Regret, grief and repentance endorse.

Privations, poverty, distress and need
Promote despair and setbacks breed,
Confusion, dismay and fears can impede
Progress in virtues and faith in our creed.

Joe Anthony

32. Love is Pain's Domain

To love you is to accept pain
From nails and thorns,
For love is pain's domain,
You, it adorns.

Your love floods our essence
Makes it refined,
Overflows in rhythmic cadence
It's not confined.

For you, one begets the other,
That's the truth,
You expect us to be together
To discern its depth.

Wrapped in the mantle of love
Embalmed in pain
We'll reflect the divine dove
It's our gain.

Joe Anthony

33. The Irony of Life

Some go through lives of toil and struggle
To amass much wealth in ways subtle
Forage for measures to make a name,
And expect all to recognize their fame.

Some aren't able their wealth to enrich
They spend cautiously to save as much,
Deprive themselves of many an essential
To equip their children realize their potential.

Most people spend their earnings on children
To educate and get degrees for their mission,
With skills and aptitudes to attain their vision,
For a future bright, with dignity and position.

Some children when they are firm on their feet
Neglect their parents, reject or mistreat,
Take life in their hands and manage all affairs,
To accept suggestions or guidance no one cares.

They dare demand their share of assets
Prefer to move out without regrets
Find a life partner and settle down far
Away from their parents' prodding radar.

They think parents are hostile and hurtful
With values and ideas outdated and awful,
They won't hesitate to take them to court
Make allegations and file a false report.

If married to an arrogant life partner
Insist their parents move out elsewhere,
Won't mind giving them up for adoption,
A home or a convent is an ethical option.

Who can imagine the anguish and pain
The helpless parents unable to constrain
Their wayward off-springs to show caring
More grateful and have the sense of sharing.

The sacrifices and misery they had endured,
Had been at intervals invested and insured
With multiple benefits in heaven's account
That will fetch them a staggering amount.

Joe Anthony

34. On a Wheelchair

Alone on a wheelchair she rested and stared,
Her look pierced the sky as its bosom bared,
Not knowing what secret held there would hurt
For she had only been seeking some comfort.

Enslaved helplessly to this device for long,
Hoping day after day to be firm and strong
And dismiss this burden and stand up erect,
Confront the world alone, daring and direct.

The car that rammed into her a year ago
Had caused her untold agony to undergo,
A lonesome widow with no one to care
Accepted this challenge without despair.

She wouldn't surrender without a fight,
This woman of mettle accepted her plight,
The words His finger wrote in the sand,
Inspired her to accept His demand.

Joe Anthony

35. Loneliness

Loneliness is a personal feeling
And a universal human emotion,
It isn't a question of lonely in being
But the traumatic sense of isolation.

Loneliness is a state of the mind
You can be lonely even in a crowd,
Or quite content when unaligned,
For it's your mind that thus avowed.

You are isolated for many reasons
For them your intentions do not matter,
You sense loneliness at certain seasons
When family or friends gather together.

Despite your many social contacts,
You are still wrapped in solitude,
Rejection and neglect are truly hard facts
Because of your negative attitude.

You may choose to live by yourself alone
Complacent about your solitary existence,
Interact with people, their outlook condone,
Broaden your horizon and avoid resistance.

Joe Anthony

36. Trgedies in Life

Tragedies in life are inevitable
They don't depend on our will,
Bring sufferings in all brutality
It's the flesh and blood reality.

Fatal affairs dreadfully torment,
For wrong decisions we lament,
Sorrow and loss of our dear ones
Or defeat of cherished ambitions.

Death may be viewed as a tragedy
Not all, but only the prematurely,
Death of an elderly is an expectation,
The death of the young is never a notion.

Loss of the knowledge and experience
We had acquired with explicit credence,
The fruit of hard work of our life entire,
In an instant is lost in the mire.

These are tragedies to mention a few
Many more can be seen in the queue
However manner we accept or react
We can't deny in life tragedies impact.

One enormous tragedy we can suffer
Is having priorities that result in failure,
And a life without purpose or ambition,
For accepting defeat is a tragic decision.

Joe Anthony

37. Despite Your Struggles

The privations and austerity you underwent,
The sacrifices you made, the hardships endured,
The grueling struggle to keep your commitment,
That was the way your success you ensured.

There is no end to all what you pursued,
To serve the needs of those you loved,
Your life's mission was thus construed,
For the benefit of them you were proud.

Times were bleak and space very dark
Life was replete with such situations,
What you felt or what you meant to ask
Couldn't ever match your expectations.

Out of love than to duty's adherence
You emptied yourself into this cauldron
To simmer in the fury of life's existence
And stand out to live by your doctrine.

Now your mission having completed
Nothing more is left for you to achieve,
Instead you ardently wish to be permitted
To retire in peace and blessings receive.

Joe Anthony

38. The Plight of the Innocent

These are just buds who gladly forego
A normal way of life to live and grow
In healthy, familiar, joyful ambience,
Unswayed by any dangerous alliance.

Most of these are orphaned by fate,
They're forced to toil day and night
In appalling conditions, most inhuman,
And held by society in isolation.

Often trapped by hardened criminals,
Operating in groups or as individuals,
Are tempted, threatened or even tortured
And are hired and their talents exploited.

These are the unfortunate little ones
Who the public discards and shuns,
Who skipped their childhood to reach a state
Where life and work would honestly relate.

They are employed in varied fields,
Over them their master great power wields,
Trafficked for pleasure or forced to rob
They're trained to excel in every job.

Their plight is mostly pain and tears,
No right to be lonely or have fears,
Uncared and unloved as rejected refuge
They spend nights in emotional deluge.

Wages are meager and often unpaid,
Amenities degrading and often delayed,
They only exist but not live as they should
As normal humans, as is understood.

Their eyes are weak, blurred and dreary,
Devoid of zest, for their life is aweary,
Their beauty lodged in each dripping tear,
That lingers at the eyelids, is true and sincere.

Joe Anthony

39. The Marginalized

They live on the periphery
Fringing the main entry,
Rejected and marginalized,
By the public are ostracized.

Alone or in groups they stay
Along footpaths, if they may,
Forlorn and dejected in spirit
For that is what they inherit.

Nothing of worth they carry,
Of vain things they are wary,
The nitwits in their bundle
They find easy to handle.

They too have varied emotions
And desire to pursue visions
But we deflect their aim
And down play their claim.

Joe Anthony

40. The Sight of Poverty

Watch that skinny kid bending down
Over a plate of food
He is struggling, look at his frown,
He finds it's no good.

His hands are trembling unable to hold
Afraid the plate might fall
By a neighbor's help he felt consoled
For he hadn't eaten at all.

He's not a stranger but my extension
But unfairly I was treating
He dies of neglect and starvation
But I, of over-eating.

Many are the gifts offered for our welfare
Not solely for us to use
Keeping things selfishly is quite unfair,
God's bounty we then abuse.

People devour food till they vomit,
And vomit to eat again.
Gluttony, a grave sin many commit
Expect God's mercy in vain.

Joe Anthony

41. Redemptive Suffering

He resembles a reed on the edge of a hill
Struggling to stay on upright and still,
Pounded by winds mercilessly cruel,
Unable to resist the onslaught that's brutal.

His creaking knees are hollow and weak,
The spine is slender, the vertebrae squeak,
He twists and turns and writhes in pain
Discreetly struggles to conceal the strain.

Transforms them into redemptive suffering
They enhance his merits and blessings bring.
He kills the power of pain in its rawness
Willingly accepts it with full awareness.

Pain can't subdue or demoralize his ego
Doesn't ask to be healed or pain to forgo,
Instead he surrenders to the Lord his agony
United with him in Gethsemane.

A whisper offers him support divine,
It upholds upright his arching spine,
He perceives the reason to regain his health
So gladly he awaits with bated breath.

Joe Anthony

42. It Was Distressing

Fifteen years they waited
To feel a rousing in the womb,
To have a new life created,
And transform their humble home.

They prayed with total trust,
God would work a miracle,
Offered prayers in earnest,
For this gift invisible.

The awakening was sudden,
The stirring in her uterus,
For life was forming within,
Their elation was glorious.

The babes emerged before time
Premature twins were they
Their gratitude was sublime
Yet tension they did convey.

The tragedy struck with the loss
Of one soon after its birth,
Held on with hope to the cross
For the other one's worth.

Having lost his brother
The younger, heartbroken,
Preferred to be together
By the Almighty's throne.

Though tragic in pain untold
The couple didn't despair,
Let God their future unfold,
Now await in silent prayer.

Joe Anthony

43. True Discernment

In gloom and darkness explore truth,
Shadows disclose life's hidden worth,
Tear filled eyes glow in joy of death,
In distress and pain the best prayer is said.

Mystery and ignorance present challenges,
Life is aware that death causes damages,
Compassion and concern, sorrow teaches
Love is the agent that mercy salvages.

In the womb of suspicion insight is born,
Silence blasts out the cry of downtrodden,
In despair fail not to shed tears of pain,
Despite all hardships hope must remain.

Longing generates joy and content,
Trepidation forges courage for combat,
Laughter prevails over fear and angst,
Doubt and distrust stir hope for comfort.

Flaws and failures proceed to success,
Struggles and hardships result in progress,
In betrayals look for trust and confidence,
Evil and wickedness will reveal goodness.

Joe Anthony

44. When Cancer Struck

It was not a shout
But a real thunderbolt
That rumbled about
By a chance default.

His fury was wild,
Like an animal he riled
That shut his reason
And his perception.

Yelling and shrieking,
In madness writhing,
He wouldn't accept
But the truth reject.

Diagnosed with cancer
No question or answer,
Refused to reconcile,
Remained very hostile.

He knew the truth,
Few days of youth
All he was given,
For death was certain.

No options left
He had to submit,
Fate was against
He knew and wept.

Helpless and distraught
Played huge tantrums,
But yielded to spectrums
That flayed his spirit.

In time he came round,
Acceptance was profound,
In humble submission
Changed his vision.

He felt at ease
In slow degrees
Stopped all resistance
Welcomed God's grace.

Joe Anthony

45. A Knock at the Door

There was a knock at the door
Gentle and soft was the sound,
I knew it wasn't a burglar
It had gentleness profound.

Hesitantly I opened the door
Was shocked to see a child,
With folded hands implore
In demeanor timid and mild.

Was she sent by someone?
I surveyed the scene closely.
Confirmed she was just one,
Catered to her silently.

She had left a shelter
Where life was unbearable
Severe was the torture
She was truly in trouble.

It's the prevalent condition
In every private orphanage,
Sickness, work, deprivation,
Subjected to inhuman outrage.

Trafficking is quite rampant,
For callous men it's a gimmick,
The helpless bear the brunt,
Truth is hidden from the public.

Such state steadily persists
Till some tragedy strikes,
Effect of the flair-up insists
Jail the guilty and their likes.

Joe Anthony

46. The Handicapped

They haven't ever played,
Never a ball they kicked,
No thrill of any victory
But a heart full of misery.

Some have no legs to walk,
Others with tongues can't talk,
For the blind it's ever dark,
And the deaf cannot hark.

A wheelchair or a stick,
Or only a pushcart to pick,
A cheap device of transport
Their only fated sport!

If there's smile on their faces
It's always tinged with traces
Of sadness for their inability
To find an end to their tragedy.

The handicap strengthens their spirits
To stand up and defy their limits,
An impetus to defend their ways
And defeat the enemy that betrays.

Sympathy and help of the public
Provide them with desired logic,
Not only to survive but to thrive
As nature wishes them to live.

An inspiration to the able,
An incentive to the ignoble,
To share the joy of the impaired,
And onward help them proceed.

Joe Anthony

47. Pain is a Human

Pain is a human,
Has a sense of humor,
Can communicate
Stories and ideas.

Can smile and laugh,
Bemoan any loss,
Listen to dirges,
Speak words of love.

Will make you feel
That you are wanted,
That all are not bad,
You have to know.

There's good in man
Even in the cruelest,
For drops can pierce
The hardest granite.

Come all and enter
The field of friendship,
Resume forbearance
Remove fear and angst.

Joe Anthony

48. Bereft of Hope

The doctor's verdict was a shock
Cancer had consumed her lungs,
He didn't talk in tongues
That suffering was in stock.

Burst into tears of desolation,
Left unable to suppress
Or her deep emotion express,
To the bed of pain, her prison.

She didn't compromise her faith
Profound was her conviction,
She knew the outcome by intuition
Yet fought for life, not death.

From a vantage point she beheld
Her cross looming up in the sky,
With hope she awaited a reply
With arms outstretched upheld.

Upon her shoulder aslant
Carried the blood stained standard,
In the two-edged sword of the Word
Her trust was deep and fervent.

Death wasn't what she desired
Time galloped like a steed
Gathered momentum and speed
To elope with her, conspired.

Her exit left everyone bereft
Though it was as expected,
Let her soul be accepted,
To the Lord is our request.

Joe Anthony

49. Healing Offers Freedom

There's a lot of hurt and pain
When healing we chose to obtain,
Freedom to maintain,
For from Sinai to Zion
Law was given to attain freedom.

When I'm inflicted with gashes and scars
Or stuck in a ditch, I lift up my arms
And gaze at the stars,
Though sin bars,
Aspire to receive the gift of freedom.

There is a purpose in pain and suffering,
Concealed from view is their meaning,
The deepest healing
Comes through suffering
That's what brings us the desired freedom.

Sign up for class in the school of sanctity,
Every course is about suffering's veracity,
Evince your tenacity
To put up with calamity
And experience healing in perfect freedom.

Joe Anthony

50. Deprivation

Deprivation is a leaking reservoir
Its performance is wayward and bizarre,
It empties all your precious belongings,
An integral part of all your longings.

Distressed at the loss of what you owned
In desolation and sorrow you then groaned,
For the time and capital you had invested
Of which you realized you were divested.

Was it the result of some sudden mishap
Or the work of a rival who laid the trap?
Whatever the cause that brought this state
You are now brought low and left desolate.

Was it a feeling of utter frustration
For your failure to accept the situation,
Or resentful questions on another's fortune
And bemoan your own forlorn condition?

Comparison creates dissention and grief,
You feel dejected and deceived, in brief,
Do not let grudge penetrate your essence
Reconcile your status with nerve and patience.

Joe Anthony

51. Not Easy to Let Go

Like a hydrogen balloon
Held by a sturdy thread
Is a charged up typhoon
Ready to explode and spread.

Wanting to surge unbridled
Like the balloon is her soul
Tries to ascend uncontrolled
The flight to reach her goal.

The thread prevents her release
To follow her aspirations
When hurdles are on the increase
She has to find deviations.

The balloon is inflated tight
Maximum space is used
Its explosion can brutally smite
The agents who are accused.

As the balloon contains a gas
That can trigger a fire
Her soul through turmoil pass
If she's to fulfil her desire.

The agent that holds the string,
Is the lure to that's mundane,
All that wealth and glory bring
She's reluctant to restrain.

She needs to let go the rope,
Allow the balloon ascend,
Freed from these, there's hope,
Her yearning to reach her friend.

Joe Anthony

52. Meet Poverty

You haven't ever met poverty
Nor tasted its unique flavor,
Your breath emits animosity
Its ethos you don't favor.

Only the poor know what poverty is,
It's their kith and kin,
They won't disown it with ease,
Though their fight is never a win.

They don't compromise their stand
Faithful to their state they abide,
Though possibilities are at hand
To upgrade their right is denied.

The poor are the people chosen
To possess and till the land,
They need to proceed with caution
And any encroachment withstand.

Joe Anthony

53. In a Quandary

The homeless man is holding a plate
In queue for an early meal is the wait,
His struggle is to sustain hope alive
And search for means his life to revive.

All misguiding scenes appeared behind,
Torturous memories held him confined
Felt himself abandon even by his own,
No one had for him any favorable opinion.

Doubted by all and distrusted by some
Dejection constrained him to stay in a slum,
Ravenous hunger like silent poison
Gnawed his dreary life in slow motion.

Wrestling with failures endured in the past
He decides his image to refine and recast,
From depression traverse a future terrain
Away from the ordinary and the mundane.
Success didn't seem to pop up its head
Grudgingly strained its neck instead,
But soon picked up speed and direction
And guided him to his dream destination.

Joe Anthony

54. Loneliness is a Predator

Loneliness is a ravenous beast
That can devour as at a feast,
Or enter the mind in gentle deceit,
A way and mode we expect the least.

It's an emotion that firmly holds,
The grip of any restraint it eludes,
In the tears of the rejected it intrudes,
In the pain of loss it silently hides.

In the empty dismal depths of caverns,
In the throes of vicious encounters,
Its ominous presence one discerns,
Causing tension of uncertain concerns.

It's around you in the fury of crowds,
In the echo of thunder of foreboding clouds,
In lonely nights of pain it abounds,
Enters your solitude without sounds.

Like liquid pain it permeates smoothly
Affecting every area of the body,
Causing havoc in the heart of the weary
Until life appears worthless and dreary.

Throbbing nerves and muscles in fusion
Pierce the aching heart to the core,
In lonesome and weary time of sadness
No one will offer to share the woe.

Wriggling in painful grip of anguish
Trying to free the aching heart,
Not knowing the strategy or the means
Life is plunged into a deep solitude.

Loneliness is an ocean of infinite pain
Swallowing up joy and satisfaction
All that's required is to swim ashore
Into the heart of human company.

Joe Anthony

III

REASON AND REALITY

Often what we observe with our external eye does not convey the intrinsic meaning which is deeper and more vital. If we delve into the bottom of these observations we will be amazed at what we discover. We will understand the reason for their existence and the meaning and value they convey.

55. Love

The word love weaves magic,
Its sound is most ecstatic,
The essence and status is deific,
Its memory is ever nostalgic.

Love's not just a feeling
It's an interior craving,
Its effect is ever soothing
And is most consoling.

Love wants total negation
Self is without position,
Rejects every opposition
Ever in pleasant disposition.

Love can bloom in every soil
Barren or black alluvial,
Concern makes it fertile
The output won't be trivial.

Love is an intimate passion
Involves trust and affection,
It's a beautiful emotion
Most profound in devotion.

Love is the glue that bonds,
Healthy friendships it dons,
To a symphony of joy it corresponds,
Hope everyone to love responds.

Joe Anthony

56. Beauty

Beauty is mystical, sublime and eternal,
Like truth and goodness is transcendental,
Beauty is holiness and spirituality is beauty,
The beauty of the cross is a scandalous ditty.

Beauty is the blueprint reflecting the divine
Communicated to the finite in him to align,
We can't teach beauty but can lead people
To experience true beauty without upheaval.

We are transfigured by sheer beauty
Like the priest's words the bread to his body,
Out of the ashes of the golden calf culture
Redemption is offered us in extreme measure.

Beauty is universal like art and music
Explosion of enchantment is often ecstatic,
When pierced by shafts of divine vision
It's the Eureka moment of recognition.

Poetry for us is the beauty idyllic
Inspirations and passion provide the basic,
It's like transition from shadow to substance,
Poetic beauty thus embellishes our essence.

Joe Anthony

57. Queen of Sentiments

Jesus used ways that seemed unusual
Called the blind man and gave him a facial
Spat on dust and applied on his eyes,
His love was in pursuit of changing lives.

Love is the most beautiful sentiment
God poured into man's heart, it's evident,
Like a sycamore that hoists a short man
To view sights he would love to discern.

Love can draw the line in the sand
As Jesus did to disperse the band,
The sinful man conceals his sins within
Only the sinless knows the nature of sin.

Only the pure knows the reality of guilt,
From others it's hidden and saved in a vault,
There were rotten fish in Peter's net
To let them back to the sea he didn't regret.

We seldom realize in wonder the view
That love is the essence of whatever we do,
When this truth aligns with human nature
It will entice us to grow up and mature.

Joe Anthony

58. Thankfulness

It is a feeling of appreciation
For a gift or service or adulation,
A thankful heart we have conceived
For favors blessed to have received.

The concept of gratitude isn't a sentiment
We could call it a virtuous element,
A quality greatly upheld by nations,
No religion will forgive its violations.

Gratitude is a virtue that shapes our actions,
Also alters our visions and decisions,
It flows spontaneously out of the reservoir
That is a constantly replenished repertoire.

Thanksgiving is a profound gesture
To God or to man, that we offer,
This feeling of gratitude is an emotion
Which results in joy and rejuvenation.

Giving thanks makes us happy and bold,
A virtue to admire, acquire and uphold,
It is not uncommon to take for granted
So gratitude must be explicitly expressed.

Joe Anthony

59. A Colorful Person

You emerge a living rainbow,
Your secrets in you are concealed,
They're for the public to know
So have them all revealed.

You are a mysterious blend
Of shades, designs and extent
Whose essence seems to defend
With pride and glory its content.

Red as blood is your passion
When love and care engage,
In orange you paint the sun
Its peel, a delicious beverage.

You spray the sky and the ocean
A soothing blue for the viewer,
You plant the meadows green
For birth and growth ever newer.

Violet dresses you a royal
With dignity, poise and charm,
Yellow is wise and loyal
Her smile is gentle and warm.

Your mantle is pure and white
A spectrum of every hue,
Indigo's brainy, has intuition,
So goes the overall view.

Joe Anthony

60. A Smile is a Blooming Flower

A smile is a bud unfolding
To become a full blown flower,
Beauty and grace diffusing
Enchanting the speechless viewer.

As its sepals open to maturity
Our lips part and cheeks bulge,
The face lights up its identity
Eyes and lips in smiles indulge.

A smile is contagious, alright,
Has power to conquer with touch,
Ease pain and evoke delight,
It costs nothing, does much.

A smile arouses vibrancy
And interest in people around,
Gives our youth primacy,
Its benefits are profound.

We were born to smile,
Began it first in the womb,
Smiling is truly universal,
In sleep too our smiles bloom.

A genuine smile has grace,
It's friendly and trustworthy,
Shares affection and peace,
Offers a sense of positivity.

Smile is a natural phenomenon
Conceals emotions of strain,
Is perennial without interruption,
So smile through fear and pain.

Smile between your sighs
When depressed and forlorn,
Penetrate your teary eyes,
And alter the sound of your mourn.

If you can only smile
When naught is deemed right,
Life is still worthwhile
Because you put up a fight.

Just like a withering bloom
Falls to the earth and finishes,
So will be your life's doom
When your smile vanishes.

Joe Anthony

61. To Have a Dream

Dreams seem mere illusions
Considered surreal delusions,
May appear to be real
But in all effect are unreal.

Some are very consoling,
Others, scary and foreboding,
Some are meant for ignoring,
Most forgotten by morning.

Dreams very often interfere
How we chart our life's career
They guide and influence our stake
And define the path we should take.

Some regard them heaven sent
And discern a divine element
We may see them in other lights
They could be mystical interventions.

Joe Anthony

62. Uncertainty

It is a brood of slithering queries,
Feeds on worms of doubt and suspicion,
Promotes and defends unscrupulous theories
And sustains polluting apprehension.

It emits defiled toxic fumes,
Basks In the hollow of perplexity,
In the abyss of confusion and qualms
Projects a chaotic complexity.

Secretes the poison of murky proposals
To be flushed into the confused brain,
Where it wriggles with possible disposals
Vitality and certitude with effort to attain.

Plodding through the desert of despair
Lost in the dismal drought of content,
Doubt is a vicious viper to compare
Lurching low as an ominous portent.

Fall not prey to its machinations
Nor to its enticing and seductive appeal,
Peep through its deceitful operations
Guard your integrity, never reveal.

Joe Anthony

63. Silence Speaks Volumes

I sat alone in my balcony
Gazing into the deep sky,
The sun was sinking well-nigh
I enjoyed my own company.

Looking into my interior
I relished my insight's flavor,
And the refreshing order
Made me feel superior.

I heard the whisper of silence
Gentle, soft and soothing,
Delicate was her essence
Her caress was peace diffusing.

Amidst numbed emotions
My waning spirit sighed,
Dreams crept in furtive motions
Searching for a place to reside.

Silence decided to shun
Sound and all such alliance
I faded into her as one,
Became a soundless silence.

Joe Anthony

64. Life Is Not a Beehive

Life's not a beehive of honey
Where you find things sweet,
Always agreeable to the palette,
Never a thing for you to worry.

It could be an oasis of illusion
Always there but unreachable,
Forces you construed feasible
Hide their heads in delusion.

Faint of heart and spirit
Your strength and energy low,
Your decisions progress slow
Resolve is a prime requisite.

Distress prevents your progress,
Everything your hand touches
Seem to move on crutches,
Your stagnant life is a mess.

Hold on to the rein strong,
Resist the advancing flow,
Defend against every blow,
Take courage with you along.

Joe Anthony

65. The Dog That Doesn't Bark

Evil is the dog that doesn't bark
But has fangs to tear you apart,
Appears at your doorstep abrupt
Concealed as a phantom in the dark.

Many are caught in its gripping clutches
Some struggle and succeed to vanquish,
Others are subdued and left to languish.
No one can ever elude its approaches.

As a guest it appears at odd times
Waits at your gate without barking,
Its growling disturbs your focus when working
So suppress and keep your mind in confines.

Evil is definitely subtle and insidious
Disguised as decent and innocent,
Deceive and manipulate our intent,
Tempt us to perpetrate acts hideous.

When passing through a somber alley
Let goodness and dignity flicker and shine,
Safety and freedom will merge and align
Your life will resemble a fertile valley.

Evil is abhorrent and vile as a viper
Thrust not your hand in its deceptive hole
It rears a brood, the same in control,
Its sting is deadlier than that of a sniper.

When you sense its putrid breath
Invoke heaven, let its aroma descend,
Then evil's essence will dissipate and end
Hold on securely to your unflinching faith.

Joe Anthony

66. Discipline Your Anger

A spark can cause a wild fire
Burn up fields of crops entire,
Turn to ashes things in its way
Spread all over in violent foray.

A spark of anger can erupt,
Like bubbling lava explode abrupt,
Turn like a raging blaze to brutal deeds,
Later shame and remorse it breeds.

If anger attacks continue to persist
Take measures to prevent or resist,
In cool demeanor expose your plight
Distract your mind with a pleasing sight.

If the fire in your belly is doused
And burning embers are no more roused,
A soothing song will calm your nerves
And heal the effects of inner maneuvers.

Joe Anthony

67. Silence is a Friend

Silence loves the hills and vales,
Showers them with warmth and smiles,
Its gentleness has a magnetic force
That can't be severed from its source.

It weaves a fleecy blanket of fragrance
To wrap them every day with radiance,
Feeds them serenity and celestial peace,
Provides a balm for tension to cease.

You don't go through sorrow or loss
Silence empties every form of dross,
Your cup is filled up to the brim
A perennial drink provided by Him.

Silence is a friend par excellence
Always adapts to its client's preference,
Tolerates tantrums and offers advice
Maintains their friendship at any price.

Joe Anthony

68. Passing Judgment

God hasn't appointed you as a judge
Why then for the fallen you keep grudge?
You are conceited and inimical
You find pleasure in being critical.

God's court is a hospice for the impious,
Not a country club for the righteous
Don't point a finger at anyone present
For then you'll be passing judgment.

Your first or last name isn't Holy
Without divine right to judge is a folly
Magdalene's accusers had dared to judge her
But to hear the lord's reply they didn't dare.

Judgment is the sole right of the Lord
He's the supreme judge of the flawed,
Judge not yourself but place before him
His judgment in your case will be a hymn.

Joe Anthony

69. Compassion

Compassion is a divine attribute
To God's compassion we pay tribute.
Feeling of pity isn't compassion
It involves a deeper disposition.

If feelings of distress at sights of sufferings
Strike vibrant chords and tug at heartstrings
Or evoke the desire to remove or reduce,
This emotion will in turn serenity diffuse.

Empathy takes its course spontaneously,
Without stifling its move intentionally,
It is ingrained in every human essence,
All it requires is a sincere acceptance.

Joe Anthony

70. Hypocrisy

Hypocrisy must be the one sole crime
Detested and despised at all time,
Masking reality with a glossy façade
To gain a popularly acceptable charade.

It implies a deception of public perception
Of desirable principles as false projection,
The image flashed is that of the Pharisees,
White-washed graves with rot and disease.

All demand approval, praise and respect,
Name and fame and power we too expect,
Hypocrisy harvests short term attraction
Oblivious of how fleeting is satisfaction.

When the disguise of dilution is exposed
And the hypocrite's true color is disclosed,
Where can he hide if his false edifice crumbled
Being deprived of the respect he'd cradled?

Joe Anthony

71. The Joy of Pardon

Forgiveness comes from an open heart,
A candid and loving trait at the start,
It doesn't endorse any preconditions,
Nor imposes any demands or restrictions.

If our hearts open with a spontaneous urge
The healing lights of forgiveness will converge,
And all the darkness within us will vanish,
No evil will linger our conscience to tarnish.

God promised that forgiveness will ensure
Peace, contentment, joy and pleasure,
Doubt not his word nor make compromise
For he keeps his promise, it's no surprise.

It isn't easy to forgive an offender
Who maligned and tore our name asunder
Humiliated us and betrayed our trust,
Schemed against us to make life difficult.

Revenge is sweet and very satisfying,
The planning to revenge is more gratifying,
Our restraining conscience holds us back
Tells of God's wrath to keep us on track.

This toughens our resolve crimes to abhor,
Gradually learn minor offences to ignore,
Forgive, no matter how grave the offence,
Peace and joy in us will be immense.

Joe Anthony

72. Mediocrity

It's a sly viper lurking furtively
In the garb of truth deceiving intently,
The state of being average or informal
And have no desire to rise above the normal.

Attitudes and habits defect our mind-set,
Lure us easily to this web of deceit,
Mediocrity condones every sin but mortal,
Remorse is a condition normal not essential.

Mediocrity draws up an unclear view
Our eyes often fail to pierce through,
The inferior motives and inadequate values
Are concealed or deleted from external venues.

It has plagued me silently for long
Till I realized here I didn't belong,
My whole system was churning within,
I felt like leaping out of my skin.

God detests every lukewarm soul,
There's no antidote except self-control,
Swallow the pride and subdue the ego,
Admit weakness and penance undergo.

Consider always excellence as a maxim,
Constant and regular at observing the dictum,
Priceless was the ransom paid in full
For God's glory then we must excel.

Joe Anthony

73. Apply Caution

Wisdom resides in the core of a person
Never on the surface makes any distortion,
If you look outside, you are a dreamer,
Looking within you makes you a redeemer.

Thoughts provoke imagination and action
They are products of fertile attraction,
Adequate results will always arrive,
Content and happiness you will derive.

The amalgam of emotions with profound reason
Is a guarantee for a successful mission,
Naught will be deprived if you apply caution,
Your progress will be driven with infinite passion.

Joe Anthony

74. To Live is to Age

Aging is a process ordained by nature,
But aging gracefully is an enviable feature
Controlled by the spirit's true perception,
And all born must age without exception.

Human beings have value and dignity
If they are productive and have utility,
If not then a worthless entity
Like a barren womb lifeless and empty.

Formerly we had an instinctive reverence
The wisdom of the elderly had deference,
The grey haired was an object of veneration,
A valuable person of immense proportion.

Old age homes is our generation's preference
Even advocate euthanasia for convenience
Caring for the old involves time and patience
So they're made to feel worthless patients.

Remember you get more than you disperse
Let their hearts in contentment immerse,
Speak to them using the language of love,
They will teach us how to suffer and live.

Joe Anthony

75. Hatred

My heart had been a battle ground
Between hate and love profound,
Hatred comes easy and spontaneous
With it revenge too is simultaneous.

Hatred is a cantankerous slithering worm
That creeps into our lives to deform,
Swallows up every portion of our heart,
Leaves no room for love to be a part.

It is a foreboding sinister cloud
That mars our vision and forms our shroud,
Steadfast love turns a mortal foe
Like virtues when mutation undergo.

Endless is the thrill and satisfaction
When hatred is replaced by attraction,
When true love reigns in regal state
And everyone holds it in high estimate.

Joe Anthony

76. Atheism

Atheism hasn't been new or strange
Has been growing wild and rampant,
Earlier there was a village atheist
But now the atheist is ruling the village.

More aggressive and overtly strident,
More pronounced and blatantly informal
Fashionable and deemed more respectable
This new phenomenon is an odious tyrant.

Happiness is one thing we want to choose
For everything else is chosen for its sake,
Immediate Happiness seems to awake
The pleasure impulses our heart construes.

When the boost of the stimulus is physical
A positive transformation often prevails,
The effect of the action publicly unveils
The experience of a joy that's transcendental.

Dwarfing reason causes mental decline,
Sweating bullets for fear of failure,
Absorbed in God's almighty splendor
The spirit will surge in search of the divine.

God gave the menu to happiness and success
Deep, pervasive, enduring in profoundness,
The Holy Spirit works in this cosmic emptiness
In the grand conspiracy of divine providence.

May God enter our brokenness with compassion,
Put a hole in our hearts to let in the Spirit
A tanker full of grace for us to inherit
And live a life with drive and passion.

Crippling and paralyzing fear of pain
Makes our hearts crave for happiness,
Trust in God is the path to righteousness,
And a glorious life is the most precious gain.

Joe Anthony

77. Odor of Peace

This scene is dear to my heart
Glowing aloud and bright
From memory it cannot part,
Fills me with fresh delight.

Imbued in awe of the mystique
In celestial splendor emerge
The tip of a lofty peak
Beyond the folded ridge.

Surveying the valley below
Bedecked with glorious tone,
In majestic array outgrow
Blossoms unique and unknown.

Fireflies tickle the sky,
In cloudless dark they fly,
Hushed in the whisper of breeze
Diffuse fragrance of peace.

Sleep beckons me with care,
Walk away I wouldn't dare,
This luring sight is awesome
In glory it appears solemn.

This picture surfaces in dreams
Gently tiptoeing, it seems,
Waving a wand in ecstasy
To offer me a valid legacy.

Joe Anthony

78. Persistence Matters

The vast expanse of the horizon
Stretching in endless fashion
From dawn to dusk
Is ever at work.

It's God's billboard that displays
The urgent messages he conveys
For us to construe
And always pursue.

We may not always understand
The meaning of his command
Which is guiding
And even chiding,

Jesus bore the fragrant load,
The tree from which he bestowed,
A progressive mission
In painful passion.

Because of the choices we'd made
Often times our intent betrayed
Our hope never died,
All odds we defied.

Wrinkles prominent adorn our brow,
Fond memories graciously avow
A story of resilience
Courage and patience.

Joe Anthony

79. Satan and Sin

Satan and sin go hand in hand
They're never divorced,
Their presence is ever in demand
Where evil's enforced.

Satan can't touch you beyond the line
Drawn by the Supreme,
But sin will drag you past that sign,
Sin's unique regime.

Sin makes a burglar commit murder
In outburst infernal,
Pleasure of sin is a fleeting intruder,
Its outcome's eternal.

Sin is potent enough to destroy you
Wages of sin is death,
If sin is forgiven then forgotten too,
You're in good health.

Joe Anthony

IV

AN INVITE TO EXPERIENCE

When we invite someone we expect them to have practical contact with facts or events through direct observation or participation. Experience helps us learn about the everyday realities of life. Life experiences are what make us who we are. Our experiences can be multi-dimensional, physical, mental, emotional, spiritual and religious, social or virtual. They shape our character and give us the capacity to handle challenges better.
Nature is the best teacher. Nature reveals the marvels of God's creation in gloriously pronounced ways. Anyone gifted with a delicate, refined and receptive mindset relishes the beauty, glamour, grandeur and spell that nature diffuses to mesmerize us. The following poems throw light on these aspects.

80. Marvels of Music

Music is heaven's melodious voice
That helps us to relax and rejoice,
Boosts our moods, rewards every effort,
Kindles vivacity and offers comfort.

Music can make us laugh or cry,
Or create the feeling of melancholy,
It drives some of our emotions and actions,
Ignites energy of pleasurable passions.

Music transcends time and space,
Cultures, nations and even race,
To human perceptions it can relate,
Positively impact our mental state.

When combined with rhythm and sound
This art creates a melody profound,
Can be recorded in a format external
In a language unique and universal.

Children learn easily by singing songs
Rhythm is a trait that to music belongs,
Dancing helps them to learn motor skills
Express themselves through pulsing drills.

When we hear a song that we like,
Our reaction renders feelings alike,
Music touches the depth of our soul
Guides us safely to reach our goal.

Listening to songs can reduce stress,
Create a sense of peace in distress,
Raise morale and improve our focus,
Make life vibrant and joyful for us.

Joe Anthony

81. Silence of the Seas

The touch of the mighty waves
In alternate ebbs and wanes
On the pebbled sandy beach
Creates an eloquent speech.

But in the midst of this sound
There is a silence profound
Only a receptive ear
Can its essence hear.

Listen to the flow of the drift
As the water leaves the coast,
The soothing echo of its silence
Will inspire you with its cadence.

Place your ear on its surface
Feel the silence of its resonance,
Get energized by the laughter
Of ripples tickling the water.

The silent words of wisdom
Are concealed in one prism,
The substance of its insight
Is sung by the water sprite.

The soothing wind creates
Gentle and tranquil waves,
Its silent tune is pleasing
And is a source of healing.

The kiss of the sun on the waters
Ushers in a glitter of colors,
Its silence is music to the soul
If your vehemence is in control.

Joe Anthony

82. Our Critical Times

As through treacherous waters we navigate
Remain steadfast and his holy law radiate,
Seek salvation in the Church, the Ark,
Before storm clouds turn things dark.

The world is sinking into an abyss of evil,
Our present time is plunged into turmoil,
Wild and barbaric their natures portray
A time of confusion and moral decay.

It is essential that we seek refuge
And shelter from the oncoming scourge,
Those who remain faithful to the Law
Shall not be swept away by the swift flow.

Immorality and evil seem to permeate,
Worshiping creatures, an act degenerate,
A fallacy buttressed by conceit and pride,
That's how God and his commands we deride.

We twist the theory of evolution to worship,
Give glory to animals, not to God's kingship,
We adore icons and venerate images
Yet reject all his divine messages.

Our visions in life and values intrinsic
Seem to have dived into chasms pathetic,
Visions of revival augur uncanny,
The only remedy is to beg to be His progeny.

Joe Anthony

83. Rainbow Rhythm

Monsoon hails us from a distance,
Without notice is quick to advance,
First a sprinkle, then a cadence,
Then in the flood you lose balance.

Stepping casually into a puddle
Can be exciting and enjoyable,
Feel the wetness hugging your bodies
Immense pleasures it embodies.

With the liquid drops as they tiptoe
Lilt and dance or do a calypso,
Sway and move to nature's rhythm
With fervor and passion infinitely sublime.

Take a stroll and regain your vigor,
To nature's sounds get exposure,
Reduce stress level and be serene,
Savor the sounds and taste of rain.

The wind winks away the dust in the air,
And its breath cools the atmosphere,
Rain water slakes the thirst of aqueducts,
Sprouting of the unborn seeds actuates.

Monsoon days are the most romantic
Make your emotions highly ecstatic
Embrace the rainbow's color and light
You'll be an emblem of everyone's delight.

Joe Anthony

84. Mist and Fog of the Wild

My elements may seem secret and mystical,
My appearance isn't physically discernible,
Colors and shades my façade adorn
Or portray an incredibly deceptive scorn.

I weave through deserts and green foliage,
Scale mountain peaks to project my image,
Measure the height of evergreen pines,
Even the depth of abysmal inclines.

My motion is a mystery even to the scholar
They gaze intently in disbelieve and wonder,
Their eyes follow the path I create
Hoping to locate and enter my estate.

How easily I elude and divert their attention
That soon they forget their original intention,
My pleasure is to confuse these erudite people
And make them believe they're senile and feeble.

Joe Anthony

85. In Your Desert

You find yourself in the middle of a desert
Where you landed without any effort,
A wilderness of sand dunes and aridity,
It's vast yet devoid of any activity.

The blaring harshness of the desert storm
Sprays dust powder, your face to deform,
Traps you helpless and blinds your vision,
Compels you to crawl against your decision.

Surrounded by scorpions, poisonous snakes
And prickly pears and cactus flakes
You search for an oasis to rest in comfort,
But an illusion is the result of your effort.

Everything seems delusional and hazy
Marred from the true nature of reality,
What you see are blurry clouds
Like a huge mass of shifting shrouds.

Can you inhale the poisonous dust,
Feel the sting of the scorching blast,
Or the sound you'd detest to hear
In the scowl of a tempest severe?

Do you have any help by your side
Or call out to someone to come to your aid?
Without any external help you are doomed
For until that comes you'll be marooned.

Joe Anthony

86. A View Through Water

I walked along the sandy beach,
On rippling waves I kept a watch,
The flow of the water in slow motion
Spoke to my heart with deep emotion.

Moving closer to the water's edge
I scooped some from the reef ledge,
It wet my palm and anointed my skin,
I felt its aroma soak within.

Sitting on a boulder I kept observing,
The smile of the moon from the depth stirring,
And stars kept winking in utter delight,
They posed for me, even gave an invite.

Skyscrapers, in bright apparel donned,
Dotted the landscape near and beyond,
Reflecting the rhythmic motion of water
Being bounced by the hand of its master.

Looking at the sky I viewed the scene
That was projected on the water screen,
The vast arched sky reflected the earth
For the same creator gave them birth.

Joe Anthony

87. What the Sky Reveals

When the sky's in turmoil and thunder rolls
And blaze of lightening our heaven controls,
God ushers forth his desire to speak,
Words of warning, often not meek.

The vast stretch of the all-pervading blue
Having hot sun beams blazing through,
Where energy and mystery were concealed
That secret message is now conveyed.

The sky is the canvas the Creator employs
On which his marvelous assets he deploys,
The solemn night sky ushers joy perennial
And the morning clouds his colors unravel.

The sky speaks for the infinity of the soul
For each seem to play a mysterious role,
Your soul, unlike the sky, is a blank slate
With inspiring words your story you relate.

Far away beyond this celestial domain
There is an awesome visible terrain
That profoundly inspires poets and artists
Dreamers, thinkers and even alarmists.

Staring at the sky restores your hope,
Connecting to nature has a wider scope,
Slows you down to opt for the best choice
And gives reasons why you should rejoice.

The twinkling tiny dots winking in the dark
Are alert benefactors providing the spark
To humans a celestial ambience to cherish,
A sanctuary for sacred rituals to embellish.

Joe Anthony

88. Nature is Awesome

I'm on a flight on wings of wonder
Gracefully soaring to dizzying heights,
Aimlessly surveying the vast blue yonder
Outlining vividly the distant sights.

Navigating the genial breeze in pursuit
I glide through some white muslin fleece,
Aiming to reach a defined target,
Down some strata of fascinating leas.

Lush green meadows of lavish space,
Decked with flowers of gorgeous hues,
Sedated and wrapped in ecstatic blaze
Descending lower was without issues.

My eyes met an impregnable fortress
Of pine trees that on the mountain fringed
Like sentinels standing erect in green dress
To salute the glorious sun as it emerged.

Above them loomed a snow crowned peak
In virginal attire with mesmerizing appeal
Pristine marvels portraying aura mystique
In ravishing rupture intoxicated my soul.

Returning to terminus I woke to reality
My soul tried to take in the new scene
The sheer experience of nature's beauty
Permeated through me and I grew serene.

Joe Anthony

89. The View from Space

Navigating a spacecraft with speed and fury
Along celestial bodies whose shapes vary
In form and dimension most inconceivable
My experience was awesome and unbelievable.

In splendor and grandeur beyond compare
Its wonders provoke us, our minds ensnare,
We're swallowed into a sphere effulgent
Enter a new world and feel triumphant.

Intense and extreme is the emotional outburst
At the majesty and the aura so august
No word can express, nor do minds construe
What lay well concealed from mortal's view.

The power and might of the Almighty
Is projected and revealed to infinity,
Anyone who can gauge its significance
Is endowed with the gift of inference!

Joe Anthony

90. The Rainbow

I'm searching for love
What is real love?
I want to get love,
And give it urgent.

My aim is the rainbow,
Its colors reflect love,
I'm searching for God,
For God is true love.

I have to know him,
Obey and love him,
That will tell me
What pure love is!

If God I can love
I can love others,
This will lead me
Back to the rainbow.

The Lord made me
A mighty rainbow,
For I'm an amalgam
Of many colors.

I can be present
On occasions and scenes,
I bridge the earth
And the infinite sky.

Joe Anthony

91. Align with Your Dreams

I want to fly with my dreams
In unrestrained abandon,
Over inconceivable themes
To experience pleasures hidden.

Swing like the blithesome lark,
On board with fairies embark
Compete with the arrow's speed
Outstrip it I must succeed.

I want to scale tall peaks,
Dive into some valley creaks
Sweep the folded landscapes,
Shout so its echo pervades.

Leap on the back of the wind
Refusing to be left behind,
Float on the speeding flow
Never a victim to lie low.

Dreams provide us visions
To pursue and make decisions,
They enhance what we're worth,
To fulfill our mission on earth.

Don't let your dreams vanish,
Lest your name they tarnish
Don't be a rudderless boat
Keep your dreams ever afloat.

Joe Anthony

92. The Writing on the Wall

The words are clear, bright and bold,
Proclaim messages that had been foretold,
Etched deeply with invisible burins
Though the wall is seen to be in ruins.

Visitors can't read as they pass by
With their alert external eye,
The letters of the words appear strange,
Can't decipher even if you re-arrange.

Close your eyes and concentrate
Let your soul's spirit communicate
The substance of the words on the screen,
The essence implied, and not seen.

It is discerned by the pure at heart
Who by virtue could claim this art,
Offer sympathy, friendship and care
And prevent anyone fall into despair.

The unseen hand that wrote the message
Owns the right to this unique language,
What is concealed within this missive
Is required to be accepted as decisive.

Joe Anthony

93. The Wild Beckons

The wild beckons me with avid attraction,
My senses ascend in profound passion,
Sights, sounds, and smells are so unique,
Their love augments my delight in the mystique.

Get near a patch of jasmine in bloom
It smells like someone bathed in perfume,
Raw soil smells of the earth's fertility
Even the hum of bees tastes like honey.

The sights of orchids dangling from trees
Are alluring scenes for stress release,
Sound of water rushing down slopes
Sentiments of sheer wonder evokes.

Gregarious birds chirping in the forest,
Smell of grass crushed under heavy thrust
Of elephant feet chasing their victim
Are all part of the age-old dictum.

The smile of the sun serves nature's needs,
Vernal pools are mantled by seaweeds,
The wild's an exotic reality to cherish,
With diverse shades of life they embellish.

Wildlife mesmerizing in might and form,
Giant trees standing like sentries in uniform,
Saluting the sinking sun as it vanishes
Invariably pleasure and joy it lavishes.

Stallions galloping in untamed abandon,
Waterfalls gushing in savage fashion,
Are sights of wonder to modify our attitude,
Still in this amalgam we'll find solitude.

Yet in the midst of all these wild scenes
We can't overlook the love and tenderness
Savage adults on their youngsters lavish
Despite their nature being fiercely harsh.

Joe Anthony

94. Hot Springs

The hot-spring is like a fountain,
Makes water bubble and spin,
Reviving and soothing by nature
It provides the required cure.

It flows fast and steady,
Cleanses the mind and body,
An incentive for the weary
Who decides to remain healthy.

It's ever clean and perennial
Some people consider it trivial
Because it's freely obtained
And the source easily maintained.

Drinking it slakes our thirst,
For skin disorder an antidote,
It is a heaven sent solution
A magical healing potion.

Joe Anthony

95. Reawakening

As my precious life mellows into evening
I take immense delight and relax
Cushioned in that soft fluffy feeling
All memories now lay under wraps.

Illusion had enclosed me in comfort
And held me cocooned and half blind,
A scene most awesome and intimate,
Mirrored a myopic view most unkind.

Fear of stretching my imagination
Beyond the borders of reason
Held me captive devoid of options
Depriving me of any honest decisions.

I lived a life that flaunts the phony,
Hypocrisy, deceit and vanity,
My life was drained of humanity,
My bearings blurred, I felt loony.

Blood, sweat and tears were required
To get me back on track for a fee,
With love and mercy the gracious Lord
Confirmed he had good hold on me.

He drew me back with the string of grace
To repent, surrender without reserve,
Bask in the sunshine of his embrace,
His forever and only him to serve.

Joe Anthony

96. Waves

Cruising on a yacht in the fading light
With the moon straining her neck to emerge,
I sat on the deck with wonder and delight
Gazing at the view the sky tried to splurge.

The rhythmic rise and fall of the yacht
Tucked at my heart in alternate cadence,
When my breathing to normalcy was brought
On the lilting waves I found my balance.

The wave was a swing that took me high
Over the horizon to unknown lands
And brought me back to reverse the try
I found myself hugged by caring hands.

The splash of colors in the evening sky
Was a living canvas of shades and designs
That made me dream of a celestial alibi
Whose genius cocooned me in gracious alliance.

All alone attuned to the seagull's call
Despite the twin engines drowning its sound
It was sheer pleasure to rise and fall
And snooze off gently in a state profound.

As darkness descended and radiance gone
With a weary heart I tore myself away
To obey the rule that allowed no exception
Hoping for such pleasure some other day.

Joe Anthony

97. We Need to Dream

Do you have dreams,
Dreams of any kind,
Dreams that provide themes
To thrill your idle mind?

Hold fast to your dream
Never let it die young,
When fading, you don't redeem
You're a bird with a broken wing.

Hold fast to your dream,
Let it not stray wild,
Be guided by its gleam
Lest your intent defiled.

Hold fast to your dream,
if you let it vanish
Life will be a dried up stream
Drought and bleakness lavish.

Hold fast to your dream
It forms life's bedrock,
Where faith and hope beam
To give you legs to walk.

Dreams define our lifeline
The fated intrinsic force
That supports the spine
For our destiny's course.

Joe Anthony

98. One Mighty Rain

It rained leaves and flowers
Withered and dried in form,
The wind had severed them
From their original home.

Soon fell heavy and hard
Fat drops of rain on the land,
Watching from my window
Felt safe my present stand.

The storm grew harsher and faster
Rode with leveled lances of rain,
Nothing could withstand its onslaught
Destruction seemed its birth right.

Water engulfed the land
But receded on leaden feet,
While nature had its pleasure
Creatures experienced torture.

Joe Anthony

99. Withered Flowers

Some flowers diffuse fragrance
Even if they wither and fall,
Their fragrance deserves reverence
For they bloomed at the creator's call.

But nobody a garland wears
Of wilted and faded flowers,
Even a new couple fears
At wedding stale flower showers.

These blossoms had their life
Solemn and glorious in time,
Like all they too had strife
But now their life is sublime

Joe Anthony

V

HEAVENLY INTERVENTION

We experience this fact in our daily lives. God's direct intervention becomes instrumental in changing some situations in our affairs. We need to speak to him and cultivate the habit of calling upon him frequently. Though he knows everything, he is never an intruder. We need divine visitation to bring the wisdom, power, favor, and blessing of heaven upon our effort.

100. Why Tie Up His Hands

We can't confine Him in a circle,
There doesn't exist any girdle
For chances of binding Him are slim,
The whole world can't contain Him.

Unfair it is to limit his work
Or the labors he won't shirk,
We'll be the ultimate loser
For he came for our future.

Our want is not restricted,
Nor future need predicted,
At others concern dismayed
We cringe and block His aid.

He goes beyond the line
No barriers for Him define,
Every frontier a beginning
And every end, an inning.

You place undue restrictions
On what would benefit others,
He removes them without delay
And leads them along His way.

Merciful and generous to a fault
He alters your closed mindset,
Until your spirit emerges
And one with Him becomes.

You hurry to open the circle
Straighten the curve external,
Your life changes for the better
And your confidence will not falter.

Joe Anthony

101. The Upper Room

Enter your upper room even by force
There to decide your action course,
Divest yourself of egotism and pride
Follow your conscience as your guide.

Your room is spacious, empty and airy,
Furnished and arranged comfortably.
Gather your friends here and deliberate,
Urge this place to sanctify and elevate.

Your room enwraps secrets beguiled
Some revealed but most are veiled
Like tongues of fire burning the curtain
To expose the essence of what is hidden.

Perform in this room crucial activities
Celebrate here your sacred festivities
Let the odor of genuine devotion
Ease and soothe every surging emotion.

Joe Anthony

102. The Good Shepherd

He is the Good Shepherd of the flock,
Sheep is his favorite of all livestock,
Lavishes love and care in abundance
Gives his life without reluctance.

Knows every sheep, by its name,
Strong or weak, healthy or lame,
They know his voice even from a distance,
At his call they around him prance.

There are no fences for their protection
So he leads them to the sheepfold direction,
They do not scatter but huddle in one place
Away from others that occupy this space.

There's no gate at the sheepfold entrance
So he lies there to check unwanted presence,
And keeps guard against wolves and thieves
Who kill or steal or commit other extremes.

He opens the sheepfold early in the morning
Calls out each name without any warning,
Gently leads them to fresh green pastures
And for a drink to some refreshing waters.

Wandering across the trackless land
One could lose way or be left behind,
He leaves the rest and goes in pursuit
Brings him home on his shoulder aloft.

Priests are shepherds of their faithful,
Who protects and defends each individual,
Drenched in the smell of their own sheep
Aspire to provide for them moral upkeep.

Joe Anthony

103. Like An Angel

Her virginal angelic face
Oozed forth blithesome grace,
My heart burst with emotion
Inspired high level of devotion.

Serenity glowed in her eyes,
Soothing was her sighs,
Her caress was sheer delight,
I was powerless to resist.

Her smile reflected innocence,
And brow of cherubic radiance
Stirred me to deep admiration,
Bringing me profound elation.

I wrapped her in warm embrace,
Kissed her guileless face,
Caressed her like a toy,
She stirred in sheer joy.

The jubilant look was vibrant,
A picture of contentment,
Flinging limbs unrestrained,
A celestial façade she maintained.

Great's a mother›s thrill
To lavish care with skill,
In adoring bond uplift
This divine euphoric gift.

Joe Anthony

104. One with the Divine

I'm grafted to God like a branch to the vine,
In the day I receive him and in worship align,
But at night within me he spiritually resides
His very presence to me succor provides.

I convert my bedroom into a little chapel,
And my bed an altar to unravel
The profound mystery of my offering
To the Divine as a victim of suffering.

It's my privilege to share his agony,
Physical, mental and emotional are many,
I make my ultimate retreat each night
And snuggle up to him in pure delight.

My sleep is serene without interruption
Wrapped in the mantle of celestial vision
Till I'm reborn to live another day
And return to the altar eager to pray.

Joe Anthony

105. A Drop of Tear

I was sitting at the foot of the cross
Pondering over the sufferings of Jesus,
Assessing how he achieved his mission
And the way he bore His final passion.

The open wound that's close to his heart
Implied an urge for love to impart,
From my eyes hot tears emerged
At the eyelid's edge they lingered.

As I felt drawn to share his vibe
And my pining his sadness to imbibe.
Suddenly a teardrop fell on my chest,
Made a scar to be my welcome guest.

Heaven was sharing my pain entire,
I dabbed the wound with the balm of desire
The rhythm of my unquenchable thirst
Was throbbing ardently in my breast.

This scar wrapped me in snug embrace,
Its soothing kiss had the fullness of grace,
I immersed myself in the waves of longing
And soared into the realm of its origin.

I entered the eye that shed the tear
And found my eternal lodging here,
Though still kneeling at the foot of the tree
My fervent spirit was blissful and free.

Joe Anthony

106. Worship in Secret

We had gathered underground
To worship in reverence profound,
Gripped by ardor and desire
Whispers turned loud from the choir.

Eyes darted around much tensed,
Glances of concern were exchanged,
A collective faint gasp echoed,
Then a muted sound followed.

A celestial radiance beamed,
Some sacred presence we deemed,
The faithful bowed in fervor
And believed they were safer.

Soon the brilliance faded,
A patch of darkness invaded
Their hearts echoed their thoughts
Inspiring were their reports.

Now we attend in secret
Firm and staunch at heart
At early hours of the day,
Resolute in faith to pray.

When secret guards relay
Warning signals that betray,
Tables are turned instantly
To avoid suspicious query.

We are the underground church
A staunch and faithful bunch
Though persecution pervades
Our faith in the Lord never fades.

Joe Anthony

107. Nobody Seems to Understand

Sitting alone at dusk at the riverfront
I watch the rhythmic pulse confront
The dormant power of the liquid below
As waves of water emerge and flow.

Throwing open my heart to the river
Trusting she would be disposed to hear,
I poured out candidly my failure and grief,
Hoping to derive some solace and relief.

She didn't seem to understand my word
There was no reaction that she had heard,
I couldn't fathom why she didn't reply
But wondered what her silence could imply.

These days the normal trend is to ignore
For nobody appears to listen anymore,
They expect you to hear what they express
For their intent is only to impress.

What you convey to receive compassion
And obtain some form of consolation
Is beyond the purview of this generation
That entertains concepts devoid of emotion.

Joe Anthony

108. An Extremely Precious Gift

Peace is a gift extremely precious
For a world of people rebellious,
The Royal Prince of Peace will enable
To restore what humans are unable.

Peace is always there free for the asking,
All around us we sense it hovering,
What we need is the right disposition,
A neutral mind receptive to intuition.

We will easily discern its object
And experience its magnificent effect
In an ambience of solemn silence
Relying on His proficient guidance.

We will perceive the hush of peace
Enwrapping us like a robe of fleece,
Genuine peace that's dormant within
Must be aroused for growth to begin.

Peace is the rustle of shriveled leaves
The tone we sense when fauna heaves,
The welcome shower of summer's heat,
And the slow descending snowflake sleet.

Peace is the aroma of morning flowers,
The meandering flow of perennial rivers,
The tranquil whisper we hear in the breeze,
And the buzzing hum of swarms of bees.

Peace is the vibrant colors of rainbows,
It is the twang of speeding arrows,
Peace is the sparkling eyes of the pure,
It's also the sober face of the demure.

Peace is the twinkle of clusters of stars
The rhythmic throb of our open scars,
Peace is the harmony of serene waves
And the warm caress of the sun's rays.

The only requisite is to have the awareness
Of the silent promptings of peace within us,
No doubt the world wouldn't only be nice
But more patently a perfect Paradise.

Joe Anthony

109. This is My Prayer

I abandoned you my Lord
Became a stranger to behold,
Went after futile pleasures,
Sin was one of the measures.

Pin prick me with your grace
Diffuse this volume of disgrace,
Drain out unchaste objects
Nothing my interior infects.

From the stable of my heart
Repulsive stenches emit
Filth my carpet profanes
From walls drip down stains.

Finally I have dethroned
Everything I had owned
Now there's ample space
So you can fill it with grace.

The little that's mine I bring
To you as one offering,
That little in your hands
Certainly increases and expands.

I'm fragmented and distorted,
My every member is isolated,
Knit these pieces together
Make this unit your treasure.

Hold me intimately close,
On you let my soul repose,
Enlarge my heart for space
All unholy agents replace.

How dare have I presumed
Without being consumed
To approach the blazing inferno
Of your presence, I don't know.

Let the burning heat of this flame
Remold my heart and reclaim,
Make it even more malleable
To bow and bend to your will.

Like Moses at the burning bush
I kneel and listen in hush
In humble adoration I bow,
A childlike trust on me bestow.

Joe Anthony

110. The Stable

He chose a stable as a home to be born
Among helpless animals cuddled in a pack,
An obscure cave, dank and forlorn,
Even the basic necessities it did lack.

Man couldn't spare a room in the inn,
Nor be present when the Lord was born,
They couldn't find any accommodation
So took shelter where animals were drawn.

No water clean, nor air fresh and pure,
Walls of the cave dripping animal urine,
Floor full of filth that's hard to endure,
Yet a straw bed they prepared therein.

Mary gave birth and laid him in a manger,
No humans present, whom he came to save,
Dumb lowly animals welcomed this stranger
A unique privilege that they did deserve.

Poverty and negation above all he preferred,
A humble disposition lowly and modest
Was an important requisite he had favored,
That would alter his followers' mindset.

Joe Anthony

111. Sancity is Not An Option

Becoming a saint is not a privilege
But a duty we know from his message,
Aiming for holiness is a universal call
Heaven is our destiny and that's final.

Just do the usual things normally each day
But do them all in an extraordinary way,
God desires we excel in modesty,
He won't be outdone in generosity.

Don't be alarmed by natural desires,
Pleasure and comfort never retires,
It's easy to flow with the tide around,
In your resistance grace will abound.

Saints were real and ordinary beings
Whose messy lives had unholy dealings,
When they realized their nothingness
With acts of love obtained forgiveness.

Like the dew dropped for the withered plants
We have been given a second innocence
Our entry into heaven will definitely be real,
Dynamic, explosive and certainly triumphal.

Joe Anthony

112. A Healing

I drank the last drop
Emptied the glass,
The dreg that settled
And weighed the most
Was the cruel agent
That killed my senses.

I sauntered unsteady
Into a land of pain,
To traverse a terrain
Bristling with spikes,
Without relief or respite
Throbbing and wriggling.

It clawed my marrow,
Pricked my spine,
Pierced my nerve
And stretched my line.
Thought end was nigh
But relief blew over.

In my dizzy state
A dew drop fell,
Smeared my face
To remove the spell,
Soothed by providence
I received deliverance.

Joe Anthony

113. He is Everywhere

His love is revealed in the eyes of a child,
Compassion in the breath of serene breeze,
His care in the wrinkles of brow is implied,
And mercy to the contrite on their knees.

His words echo in enthralling cadence,
In the whirring tone of the bee hummingbird,
Tiniest though, it exerts much influence,
An ensign to lead the sad and defeated.

His tears downpour in unending torrent
Nonstop without reducing its quantity,
Lavishly generous is his endowment
His largesse offered to the seeking entity.

His face reflects a withering flower
Struggling to survive the onslaught of heat,
His glory explodes to grant us the power
To confront the evil and force it to retreat.

His passion is veiled by the mask on his face
Disguising the harrowing pain he bore,
Purging all those who wish to embrace
And hold on to him to heavenward soar.

Joe Anthony

114. God Wrote My Story

God has started writing my story
Know not if that'll bring me glory,
I can't read for I'm nearly blind
In time I know the truth I'll find.

He weaves events one after another
Merges images and citations together,
The final outcome will everyone astound
Because the contents are true and profound.

Many won't know what's hidden within
The wreckage of life that once was mine,
It could turn out a source of hope,
To uplift the fallen there could be scope.

Despite the weight of the burden I bore
And the consequences I couldn't ignore,
Emerged within me a pleasant scene,
That brought me feelings sober and serene.

My disconnect with the Lord was the cause
Of walking in circles without remorse,
Fearing my failure to follow the source
Leading me directly to the foot of his cross.

The best of things come through loss and pain,
When on wheel-chair our hopes remain,
Despite situations sordid and grim
The only antidote is our trust in Him.

Pull back the curtain and unveil the truth
That's concealed from the aged and the youth,
Going by feeling is a treacherous response,
Strike at the core to obtain the essence.

There is an entrance that's purely mine
Only the author can choose and assign
To anyone for access to this story written
By the hand of God, for it was his mission.

Joe Anthony

115. On the Wings of Prayer

When we take our infant step to sanctity
It's the start of a long strenuous journey,
Through ups and downs we may traverse
And often encounter situations averse.

God props us up where we least expect
That's unfamiliar and uneasy to accept,
We must walk down the road of prayer
For without that there's no getting there.

We could take the trail transcendental
And unwrap the mysteries under veil
Or choose a track that's easy to tread
And proceed at our own pace instead.

Whatever be the choice we make
Will be for holiness for His sake,
For he called us purely to this end
So there's no reason for us to pretend.

Our ears attuned to celestial music
And our soul enthralled and ecstatic
We precede steadily emitting rays
From sparks of truth and love's blaze.

Let the delightful laughter of breeze
And rapturous songs of birds and bees
Gift-wrapped in one throbbing cadence
Resound as echo in profound reverence.

So shall our holiness blend and unite
As one unique essence of a divine rite
To offer in oblation with the Most Holy
And be redeemed and crowned in glory.

Joe Anthony

116. Surrender All

God invades our comfort zone
Shakes us up and rattles every bone.
In the struggle for spiritual progress
Wants us surrender all we possess.

He knows we are broken and scattered,
Messed up, frightened and even scarred.
Full of stains that need to be purged
And unholy habits casually surged.

We must unmask and reveal to the Lord
Secrets stored in our subconscious record.
The heavy burden of worries and cares
Can be overcome through fervent prayers.

Despite His majesty and immensity
He lowers Himself to us with humility
Smoothens the blunt edges of our heart
He wants blessings and grace to impart.

He binds up wounds with compassion,
Tenderness, patience and affection,
Offers living water to slake our thirst
His body and blood to nourish our spirit.

Why in the end we can afford time
For everyone else, but not for Him?
We should be before him on our knee
Kiss His feet and be like Magdalene!

Joe Anthony

117. The Fig Tree

This fig tree wasn't fecund
For on it no fruit was found,
The owner was utterly dismayed,
Its felling was then ordained.

The gardener's benign nature
Urged to reconsider the matter,
And another chance to offer
If the laborer would do better.

God is the soul's gardener
And even so a partner,
He's at work as ever
To bring out our best with honor.

Joe Anthony

118. The Transfiguration

Brighter than the sun his face was radiant,
In dazzling white sparkled his garment,
Revealing a glimpse of his glory and majesty,
For the three knew it wasn't a fantasy.

Moses and Elijah of the ancient rite,
Many eventualities and failures despite,
Revealed the continuity of the salvific plan
God had been pursuing since time began.

Peter suggested they build three cabins,
For such an occasion, as everyone imagines,
But the Father's words from the dense cloud
Was a clear command that echoed aloud.

The three disciples stooped in devotion
Listening to the words, "He is my son
In whom I'm pleased, to him you listen".
An experience they have never forgotten.

Joe Anthony

119. Door to the Next Room

Come my dear soul you and I
To the next door let's draw nigh,
Knock gently for a quick reply
On which we can certainly rely.

He's there waiting, have no doubt,
In our demeanor let's be devout,
The room is the foyer to his shrine,
On his throne we'll meet the divine.

Death is the door that keeps us apart,
Only a step away from the start,
Quick and smooth will be our last sigh
Between death and rebirth there's no bye.

Joe Anthony

120. Sudden Awareness

Have you ever come across as a sleuth
Wherein you suddenly realized a truth
That was there all the while in all vigor
Yet never made your attention trigger?

Then in the flicker of a moment it emerges
Across your horizon suddenly it flashes,
This instant realization evokes pleasure,
Or intense shock of an extreme measure.

Won't you yell out why you missed the fact,
That didn't enter your survey intact,
And accuse yourself of a lack of interest,
Decide to fortify your waning mindset?

This is common in the lives of most people,
Some view it ordinary, normal and casual,
Others discard it as futile and ridiculous,
Spending time on such seems frivolous.

Joe Anthony

121. The Chosen People

The children of ancient Israel
Yahweh's chosen people,
Were freed from bondage
Which was their heritage
In the great Pharaoh's Egypt.

He led with deeds mighty
His men to a land of plenty
Flowing with milk and honey
Blessed all of them immensely,
Protected and dearly loved them.

Despite failures repeated
He forgave all who repented,
In their own land they settled
Had them in his nest nestled
And destroyed their enemies.

I too am a chosen,
Given faith and reason,
That our fathers had won
By trust and true devotion,
In my heart it's a treasure.

A reason sufficient enough
To forego every rebuff,
And cherish this priceless belief
That I'm God's anointed puff,
Blessed be the Lord our God.

Joe Anthony

122. The Tiny Sparrow

Like the sparrow that found a shelter
And built its nest below the altar,
Housed its nestlings in safety and solace
I too found a congenial surface.

Cradled in a warm and gentle hand,
The loving hand of our dearest Lord,
Though feeble, frail and weak I be,
I can observe and things foresee.

There's no frontier I can't cross,
Nor any ocean I can't cruise,
No mountain that I cannot scale,
Because I have the Divine seal.

I had lived through complex times
And have suffered untold pains,
Feared to raise my wings to flutter
As my feathers were in need of succor.

The gentle rays of the Divine Son
Warmth infused, and healing done,
Regained strength of my faltering wings
To enable my soul to sing him hymns.

From a mundane podium he launched me
Into his treasure house to be a trustee
Unlike the sparrow, that tiny bird,
Now a mighty eagle I'm transformed.

Joe Anthony

123. The Book of My Heart

On a white sheet in my heart
I scribbled a rough note,
An account of my losses
Ink crimson red, in doses.

The losses were heartaches
Offered as keepsakes,
Clobbered by rejection,
Insult and exclusion.

A brown page of the mind
With skeletons outlined,
Tortured me ruthlessly
And rejected me utterly.

The red page was pain
That stabbed its domain,
Fragmented its frontier
In torments severe.

The black sheet eclipsed
My innocence, and stripped
My brilliant script,
I was left bereft.

Every page portrayed
Negativity, and conveyed
That futile was the dream
I'd tried to redeem.

The losses assured me,
Announced a guarantee,
A reward for my offer
Of total surrender.

There's ache in love
As taught from above
When love generates pain
It's a mighty gain.

Joe Anthony

124. A Nightmare

She presented a strange sense of secrecy,
Appeared to possess a protective aura,
And an eerie and enigmatic persona
Which intrigued me to unravel her mystery.

Stepping into an unknown territory
Uncertain of what I would uncover,
An unsettling thought blew me over
I couldn't fathom her tragic story.

A scary dread targeted me to enslave,
It was beyond any human conception
The air in me was thick with tension,
Panic spread through like a tidal wave.

I struggled in despair to breathe as normal
But the choking condition offered no relief,
I tried with all effort to suppress the grief
A relentless struggle of good versus evil.

An underlying current of terror took root,
A cold wind swept through me chilling my bones,
A hot sweat dripped in groans and moans,
It was more like two dislikes in pursuit.

A voice then whispered in the stifling silence,
It was a soothing balm amidst the storm,
Its echo helped all energy to transform,
The situation improved under its guidance.

The silence in the room was almost visible
Then each word seemed to reverberate within
With faith as shield and prayer as weapon
A flickering light brought about this miracle.

Joe Anthony

VI

REMINISCENCES

We love to recall incidents, experiences, or feelings from a remote past that are usually pleasant and share them with others. It aims to evoke memories, stimulate mental activity and improve well-being. It is often assisted by props such as videos, pictures and objects. Reminiscing restores our sense of self and belonging and brings us joy. It helps us cope with growing older as we recreate our life's meaning by being connected to the past. It also helps reaffirm our feelings of being important. Besides, sharing the past helps seniors reflect on their achievements and appreciate what they have done. This is what these poems claim to reflect on.

125. Remembering Antoinette

She was simple but elegant and graceful,
Deeply religious, devout and faithful,
A woman of principles and positive outlook,
To tarnish her image I would never brook.

Sincere, honest and serene in demeanor,
Was known for her impeccable character,
As a person she had dignity and poise,
Was a good singer with a melodious voice.

Tasteful and flawless her sense of dressing,
Attracted people for her impressive bearing,
Humble by birth but of noble attitude
That's how I met her who altered my solitude.

Hers was the one heart that beat with mine,
The loving, sincere, delicate and pure,
Like enticing drops of seasoned red wine
Offered in abundance as a remedial cure.

Hers was the arm I clung to at each step
When years drifted by and life grew grim,
On her shoulder I leaned often for help
She was the buttress, like a comforting hymn.

An excellent cook who could turn out dishes
Delicious to the palate according to our wishes,
For she loved cooking, it was her pleasure,
Her mother's gift she cherished as a treasure.

She was a teacher before her marriage,
All household affairs she was trained to manage,
A wonderful wife and an affectionate mother,
Above all a friend, who knitted us together.

With needle and thread she created beauty,
Skillful with fingers she made it her hobby,
Took all pains and went through humbling days
To augment the income for life's standard to raise.

Fond of reading and watching television
Were her other pleasures that broadened her vision,
Always stood by me in all my decisions
With support and urge, and laid no conditions.

A devout catholic regular at daily Mass,
Praying the beads and special Novenas,
Offering a monthly Mass for the Souls,
These had been some of her characteristic roles.

She suffered much as a chronic diabetic
And related illness that proved tragic
One sad day she went, left us in the bargain,
Never wanted to be a nuisance or a pain.

Joe Anthony

126. Ever Enduring Memory

Your memory is like the fragrance of the incense
That rises from the altar and reveals its presence
Bequeathing a gift in deific eloquence
To all your devotees who vow you adherence.

But only a whisper taps at my deaf ear
What you desire to convey isn't clear,
Are you undecided or reluctant to interfere,
Should I in confusion before you appear?

Even though your heart is burning as a beacon
My eyes are dim, my mind cannot reason.
I fail to hear you or see you as a falcon
Of divine love, though definitely you're one.

You have turned off the light from my vision,
To draw me closer did you make provision?
It's my faith that prompts me to petition
And cherish your memory forever in elation.

Whenever my distraught heart on you relied
I felt your presence over me preside,
Attend to my prayer now and succor provide
For firmly I believe in God you abide.

Your eloquent silence is truly effective,
The brilliance of your eyes is genuinely reflective
Of what you've in mind, for you are receptive
To all our requests, and deeply attentive.

The smile that beams on your seraphic countenance
Echoes your reply in profound resonance,
As delight and content are in ardent romance
No effort is needed your concern to enhance.

Joe Anthony

127. Longing for the Mountains

A pensive sadness pervades my being
Seeps through the marrow of my spine,
I feel its effect gently beckoning
Urging me proceed to a scene benign.

An aura of mystic silence and peace,
Whose presence I am unable to resist,
Draws me closer offering release
From tainted images that still persist.

Jesus would often slip out alone
Tracing the winding mountain road
To sit with his Father by his throne
And lovingly before him his mind unload.

I want to tell him so many things:
My hopes, sorrows, fears, anxiety,
Secrets, desires, failures and pains,
And live with the One who owns eternity.

To sit by his side and sense his breath,
Inhale the aroma of his whispers of care,
His mystical touch of celestial warmth
Oozing copiously with me to share.

He is Love, the answer and solution,
I profess him love like no other does,
He engulfs me in his prodigal vision
I melt into him as he wraps me thus.

What an abode to recline and rest
Leaning on him with firm confidence,
United with the love of my quest
Within the heart of peace and silence.

Joe Anthony

128. Good Old Days

I feel nostalgic about my earliest years
When the family would kneel before the altar
To pray every evening before our supper
The Angelus, the Rosary and the Psalter.

A lonely candle the prayer room hallowed,
Where divine images were ever revered,
Hymns were sung and Scripture was read,
To conclude the day long toil and sweat.

After the supper mother would read
Stories of saints which we eagerly heard
Cried or laughed with her as she reacted,
Promised to imitate the virtues proposed.

Soon the ecstatic feelings would decline
Our senses derailing our attention span,
Mother would plant a kiss on our cheek
As she blessed us for a peaceful sleep.

Joe Anthony

129. In God's Abode

I hear a hushed and mournful melody
Weaving through a mesh of colors,
The scene and occasion is an elegy
As the sun sets beyond its borders,
It's a son's dirge for a loved mother
Who had left him for her maker.

She'd lived long and toiled hard,
Enjoyed little and suffered a lot.
A wonderful wife of high regard,
A model mother who happiness brought,
A holy woman, a true believer,
Par excellence as a generous giver.

Her life was full of struggle and stress,
She offered herself as a votive victim
On the altar of pain and loneliness
For she thought it right, in her wisdom.
Written in blood and tears of grief
Bringing up seven sons was no relief.

Life was hard but there was joy
In their littleness and meager means
At their disposal they could employ.
With time, sons grew beyond teens,
Found employment and got married,
To greener pastures they hurried.

She felt a cold and empty void,
A time of loneliness and distance,
She was not ever alone or neglected
There was at hand all assistance.
At times she felt some rejection
Or lack of care and protection.

Her final days brought peace and grace,
With weak and fading look she smiled,
Her fragile frame and wrinkled face
Had the innocence of a sleeping child.
A life well spent as God had ordained
Was prepared herself to meet her end.

Then one day when all were in dismay
She waved her eyes to farewell convey.
She looked at those, gave a warm smile
And sailed away leaving a worthy profile.
Today at her grave endowed with grace
I felt her breath caress my face.

Joe Anthony

130. Nostalgia for My Childhood Home

I feel nostalgic for the lush green landscape,
That ambushed my memory, prevented escape,
It is now vibrant and striving to emerge
As my hazy mind weaves through that foliage.

I was intrigued by the presence of the flora
And mesmerized by its magical aura,
For their beauty, colors and fragrance,
Have seeped into me in refreshing radiance.

Fascinated to observe the butterflies kissing
And sharing secrets with the flowers and wishing
And gliding over in glorious elation,
Aiding the process of pollination.

Honey bees frequenting flowers in bloom
And buzzing back hastily each to its room,
Squirrels endlessly chasing each other
Unalarmed by the presence of any onlooker.

Mother birds picking food for their young ones
That stretch out their necks at the nest's entrance,
Their incessant chirpings are melodious calls,
And the sight of their colors enraptures and enthralls.

Soft and smooth is the feel of the breeze
That blows at dawn and caresses my cheeks,
The sun winks and peeps through porous clouds
Carving out designs in awesome shades.

In the richness, beauty and mystery of nature
My spirit penetrated the essence of this picture,
Gazing at the celestial terrain in wonder
Engulfed by silence I met my Creator.

In nature's untarnished virginal grandeur
This was a fascinating and stirring encounter,
The tantalizing glimpses of God's glory so august,
Evoked a desire to offer myself as a holocaust.

Joe Anthony

131. Redeemed

When I was young and disconnected
I went after the sophisticated,
Snobbish and conceited was my stand
I avoided the mediocre and the bland.

Now I prefer the simpler kind
Rich or poor I don't mind,
Fairness in all dealings is important
Irrespective of results they represent.

I wish to forgo things and proceed
Become poor and experience need,
Share what I have with the have-nots,
For love and acceptance it connotes.

Share with the needy was his decree
Then we don't have any right to disagree,
Humbly submit our decisions to his will
Leave the all rest for him to fulfill.

Joe Anthony

132. A Lost Past

I sat somberly on a river's edge
My dangling legs sensed its wetness
My lonely heart was a willow of sadness,
I seemed unable to fulfill my pledge.

A torrent of turbulent and painful memories
Suppressed by fated circumstance,
And artificiality endorsed by distance,
Erupted in fumes of emotional fantasies.

Sad beads brimmed my hazy eye,
To blur my vision of those I loved
The status I had earned and held,
All now a lost past, I wanted to die.

The tide toyed with empty cans,
From which life had drained out.
I was a straw in the flood of fate
Lashed about by the river in rants.

Tossed against the distant rocks
Countless times and unabated
I rose and fell being unaided
A non-entity, much like a copse.

I rose upon two staggering feet,
The world reeled in frenzy upbeat,
My dreams all turned utterly bitter
And I realized kisses here blister.

Then a joyous song my heart hummed
It kissed a bud, instantly it bloomed,
A smile filtered onto my strained face
And brought my hope to the surface.

Joe Anthony

133. My Sun is Setting

Even when life is mellowing in age,
My spirituality is an infant to gauge
My devotion is dwarfed to a low grade
What's crucial is my worth to upgrade.

Gentle and meek was my early childhood
The contours of my spirituality then curved
Like a plant bent when trying to sprout
Beneath a rock in the winter's drought.

Care wasn't taken, wayward I moved on
Aimlessly carousing from night till dawn,
Till age caught up with me never to let go
Compelled my growth in holiness forgo.

Spirituality is an early phenomenon
Among simple and ordinary men,
I am one of those who realized late
The value of holiness, it was my fate.

Lord I need help for time is very short,
My urge to approach you do not abort,
I'm craving to perform something drastic
That will lead me to a vision ecstatic.

Confused and lost, I cannot concentrate,
With a contrite heart at your feet I prostrate,
Only my trust in your mercy can redeem me,
Uproot and replant in heaven this old tree.

Joe Anthony

134. At Their Grave

My spirit is hovering over the grave
Where my parents have been buried.
They lived as one, as one now rest
Though they left us nine years apart.

Their bodies are no more present here
But the tomb emits the unique aroma
Of the living presence of these two souls,
To remind us that they are with us.

The principles and values they had cherished,
The exemplary manner of life they lived,
Their love for God and for his commands
Are for us all to absorb and emulate.

As I stood in silence at their resting place
A gentle whisper of love reached my ears
Their soft voices had a joyful tone
It was their prayer for the salvation of my soul.

Though no flowers are strewn at their grave,
Nor any candle glows in the day or night,
My love has weaved a wreath of blessings
Entwining them into one eternal unit.

The ambrosial scent of our frequent prayers,
The Holy Masses offered on occasions,
And the light of candles burning on our altars
Are still enshrined around their grave.

Life has mastery over death is the truth
Even though death seems to subdue life,
They're alive and at home with the Lord,
Their precious memory can never be erased.

Joe Anthony

135. Those Were the Days

I wandered about down memory lane
Barefooted in reverie serene and sane,
Kicking at random dry leaves of events
Scattered about in lethargic intents.

Those early years were devoid of strain,
Casual and informal in attire plain,
Picking up fights or settling disputes,
Hiding from parents ungodly pursuits.

Hunting for eggs in concealed nests
In thickets and shrubs away from pests,
Skipping over fences in the middle of the night
To pilfer rare fruits seldom in sight.

Hook a fish or two, or hunt a duck,
Often brought home something at dusk,
Played truant to watch action movies
Pockets filled with delicious chewies.

Our pranks were simple without guile
Innocent in tone was our lifestyle
Love and obedience with a splash of care
Marked our life with work and prayer.

Joe Anthony

136. She Dived Into the Foam

On life's barren threshold she lingers
Peering through bleak and dismal haze,
At this dreadful scene her decision falters
Her love was swallowed by fierce waves.

With sad and frightened eyes she mourns
Surveying the wreckage that is adrift
Where the water seethes and scorns
Shattering every fiber of her heart.

She hears him in the whisper of the wind
A dejected echo of his struggle with death
Weeping and sighing seems to make her blind
But feels his shadow stalking her breath.

She reads what lies between the lines
Deciphers what her future upholds
Waddling down with the wreckage she aligns
Dives into the white foam that her enfolds.

Joe Anthony

137. A Bereaved Father

O gentle primrose delicate and sweet
Bloomed in our garden of love
You tarried not your father to meet
He wasn't near enough.

I yearned to skip over mountain peaks,
Bore through clouds of snow,
Break dense walls with harshest shrieks
And fly across valleys below.

I kept count of the days lamenting
Sore, distraught and helpless,
Barracks held me from duty flouting
Waited for leave, restless.

The delay pierced my impatient heart
Wanted you in my arms,
Hug you and never ever let you part
Now I'm having qualms.

The most heartrending news was relayed
Across the squadron quarter,
Sorrow and loss on me heavily weighed
Broke my heart by torture.

Your death broke my heart asunder
Shattered my every dream,
Having my right see suffer plunder
Wanted your name to redeem.

I can never know how you smiled,
Nor sang or cried or played,
Your look could erase my pain dear child
Had your departure been delayed!

The dithering to arrive wasn't my choice
Things here are quite impersonal
In your memory we shall ever rejoice
Lighting an unfading candle.

Joe Anthony

138. Winds of Change

He wasted his life on futile stuff
Wandered about aimlessly,
Day and night his life was tough,
Begged for help shamelessly.

An old man offered him night shelter,
He was a man of compassion
Though a shrewd financial investor,
A quality rare in fashion.

Worked for his new benefactor
Began to earn merit,
Soon he started a new chapter
Became a partner with credit.

Ever a loyal and sincere escort
To his boss and friend,
In prosperity and exceeding comfort
Lived to a splendid end.

Joe Anthony

139. When I Leave You

I'm spending life on a ventilator
Awaiting relief from an impending danger,
Before my life goes dysfunctional
Just a few things to you I want to tell.

I want you, if possible, at my bedside,
To assure you in my love you do reside.
Remember and pray for me after I'm gone,
At my departure you shouldn't mourn.

I wonder how my face will appear,
When sent to my friends as souvenir,
I'm certain I'll be close to your heart,
In offering prayers for me you'll take part.

When you post of my death to my contacts
And apprise them in time with all the facts
Convey my love and bid them farewell
Tell them I left for home with my angel.

I want my funeral to be simple and low
There won't be many whom we'd know,
Bury me, if possible, in my wife's grave
And on our tomb stone my name engrave.

Joe Anthony

VII

HOPES AND EXPECTATIONS

Surprise and shock are emotions that strike us at unexpected moments and we are startled and disconcerted. We could experience instant surprise, pleasure, doubt, despair or grief. Life is full of unexpected emotions and events. In this section we shall dive into some situations and events, people and objects to encounter unexpected truths.

140. Burst of Dawn

Today at the burst of dawn
Clouds in clusters adorn
The mesmerizing blue dome
And in blithesome passion roam.

Dew drops falling on leaves
Caressed by gentle breeze
Blow over opening buds
Eager to welcome with hugs.

Waltzing on tiptoe the odor,
Lilting and swaying in candor,
Galvanize nature's spirit
To soar high beyond limit.

The smile of beaming sun rays
Signal the promised grace
Blending with love and praise
Offered to our human race.

Joe Anthony

141. A New Universe

I am in search of a mystical universe
Where its roots spread in directions diverse
Envelopes a world in fantasy to nourish,
Permits all forms of delight to flourish.

I want to dance on rhythmic waves,
Enjoy the magic food everyone craves,
Escape to a world of silent meadows
Or repose within the womb of shadows.

Come with me to this fantasy wilderness
We'll be wrapped in the mantle of tenderness,
Our new world will have the ecstatic perception
Of a fruitful life beyond any deception.

Joe Anthony

142. Paint Me a Colored Dream

My dreams are often grey and bleak,
With appearance distorted and freak.
I am unable to decipher their content
Nor appreciate the message they intent.

Paint me dreams in colors bright
Distinct, graphic with clear insight,
Of scenes of delight, beauty and grace,
And people, angels and fairies in space.

Dreams of mist and dew and breeze,
Green meadows live with birds and bees,
Rivers meandering down narrow creaks,
And rainbows bridging mountain peaks.

Paint me dreams of smiles and cries,
Of pain, compassion, love and largesse,
Paint me dreams of genuine forgiveness
Using colors of warmth and thankfulness.

I want my dreams to be active and alive
Diffusing light with pep and drive,
Paint for me the dream, the one ultimate,
When in the divine bosom I find rest.

Joe Anthony

143. A Conspiracy

The sky had dropped its nocturnal curtain,
To blink or not, the stars were uncertain,
Voices of the night weren't heard or silent
Any form of motion was unseen or absent.

As I lay on my couch for rest and relief
Creeping fibrous tissues of grief
Were cobbling together loss and pain
To cripple and inert me furtively within.

My spine was tethered to the stem of time,
With harrowing feeling, when committing a crime,
Burrowing traumas deep down my throat,
My sinking heart was struggling to afloat.

Unholy elements all seemed to conspire
To support their ravaging greed to acquire
The peace and pavilion that had been mine
And use their power my status to undermine.

Detecting their intent I applied caution,
Planned out all possible defensive motion,
With vigor and resolve I could implement
Avail the Lord's grace chip in to supplement.

Joe Anthony

144. Being Alone

Some would prefer to live all alone
To appreciate humanity all the more,
When we're alone we see true beauty
Appreciate goodness more like a duty.

Loneliness brings out the best in us,
Our creative mood, to work it does,
God uses to advantage our loneliness
For loneliness isn't a death sentence.

Be grateful for the chance to be alone
It's the time to be a part of his mission,
He wants to be intimate with me and you
He has feelings of love for us too.

If we don't consider him as our strength
We sure are not on the same wavelength,
If our flaws and failures are revealed
In his presence we will be healed.

Joe Anthony

145. Rumination

Come my dear soul, let's go far
Beyond the narrow ridge afar,
Sit on the bank of swollen river
Dangle our feet in its cool water.

Its cleansing freshness will revive
Our dejected spirit to help us survive.
Our mind is a sea of turbulence,
And heart a volcano of violence.

Let the impact of this serene set
Guide us to ruminate and digest
Why he's stubbornly playing God,
When he knows he's trapped by pride.

His swollen ego is deflated,
And his mind-set disoriented
Rates honesty and humility as foes
He won't relent, nor will he pause.

He's determined to be his own savior
Wants to flow with the tide or sink deeper,
End in the abyss of despair and gloom,
Wrapped in silence and solitude assume.

He can't bridle the lure of addiction
His heart will pronounce his own conviction
No choice but accept the inevitable
That destiny will place on his table.

Joe Anthony

146. Complement

People are weary of offering complements,
They keep it locked up as precious contents
For fear they offer it in the absence of desire
Or it slips out when their hearts are on fire.

You lose nothing when you do acknowledge
The meritorious action offered as a pledge,
The thrill and elation derived from this deed
Lasts a life time, for it is guaranteed.

You don't lower you status or vision
If praising someone is your decision,
Your status increases above the normal
You are admired and considered cordial.

Appreciation and complements are divine features
Always rewarded by heaven and its creatures
So be profuse in your praise for the doer
Lag not behind to step forward and offer.

Joe Anthony

147. Beware

My boat's afloat on a leisurely cruise
Its silky sail flutters in the wind.
I've no care in the world to mind,
No worries to disturb my quiet snooze.

Like feathers that drift and glide
A gentle slumber caressed my soul,
Peace and serenity wrapped my whole,
But this wounded Satan's pride.

He stirred into action, raised a storm,
Battered my boat with raging waves
Against a rock that struck the base,
My sail in shreds, couldn't perform.

An agonizing fear gripped my heart
As I went down I yelled in agony,
An extended hand reached out to me,
Drew me up then saw him depart.

Filled with awe and deep reverence
I recognized the scar on his palm,
That gripped in time my shivering arm,
On my knees I paid him obeisance.

Joe Anthony

148. See Things in Color

We should view the world in color
So too every expressed gesture,
Not every negative represent a sin,
A unique depth and mass they bring.

If we encounter a mystic force
Drawing us to an inward course,
Hold on to the supernatural rope
For deliverance, still there's scope.

Are we like birds whose wings were clipped
And couldn't take off when we wished?
God will show us a realm more real
And give new wings to face the ordeal.

God intercepts time and space
To reach our hearts with his grace,
To spend our days one after another
As on beads we pray and ponder.

Our new world is the secret of the spirit
Awaiting us to discover and inherit,
Gives us the lifeline to heaven ascend
Until our journey comes to an end.

Joe Anthony

149. Search Your Heart

My heart has been locked
And for some time sealed
Afraid to open its entrance,
It's fortified to be a hindrance.

I fear encountering elements,
Sinister and foreboding regiments,
Deep in my heart's crevices
Settled without my awareness.

Concealed culpable deeds,
Fresh and hurting wounds,
That I may by force divulge
To discredit me they indulge.

Embarrassing memories emerge
Cluttering the precious space,
Only infused grace divine
Can redeem me and refine.

Joe Anthony

150. Enter His Orbit

We offer to God our ventures of each day,
The hardships we endure along the way,
The ups and downs we grapple with
And the pain that penetrates our depth.

We include the fantasies that assail us,
The unholy thoughts and sordid desires
That coil and recoil in our complex mind
Along with fears and frustrations combined.

Let these with our prayers within,
Revolve around the Eternal Sun.
We also include the bundles of joy
And gifts galore, to cherish and enjoy.

The profound bliss dropped into our cradle,
The loaves of comfort set at his table,
The fistful of success he lets us attain,
When we thought we'd struggled in vain.

Look not back at the sins of the past
Into his furnace of love have them cast,
Where they are consumed leaving no trace
Freed from remorse and granted grace.

Keep our body erect and look ahead,
Revolve around this Sun instead,
And rotate with him on a sacred journey,
To enter his orbit we'll be made worthy.

We shall move with our vision un-blurred
Blissfully above the rest of the world,
Become renewed and immersed in him
And be found deserving to offer him a hymn.

Joe Anthony

151. Always Look Ahead

I scaled the staggering heights
By a narrow ladder that unites
The earth and sky in firm grasp
Bound securely by a strap.

Steep and narrow in appearance
There were no reasons to fear,
Its swaying was of no concerns
For their ends did well adhere.

Viewing from aloft at the chasm
Can ruffle our nerves to panic
And cause a muscular spasm,
A reaction that could be tragic.

Looking up gives an impulsion
To proceed ahead with trust
Expectation in full eruption
Helps our mindset to adjust.

Joe Anthony

152. Get Down to Reality

Breezing through a clump of fluttering feathers
My soul perched on a twig of emotions
Listening to the cry of unseen creations
Trapped in cages or bound with fetters.

Shadows of phantoms on waves of loneliness
Are spinning a web of mystical desires
To infuse this surreal world that conspires
To project a physical outlook of normalness.

My angst at confronting vagueness of purpose
Explores further deep the core of fantasy
To discern veiled clues parading aimlessly
That provoked my concern for this futile pose.

Life in the abstract and intangible sphere
Devoid of substance and shapeless in form
Creates distrust and doubt as being the norm
So from fancy to matter I was made aware.

Joe Anthony

153. Selected Wisely

Two roads diverged in a yellow wood
We hesitate to choose to advance ahead
We knew we couldn't traverse both
Deep in thought we took our oath.

I decided to take the winding one
Though it seemed to need tough action
He looked down and liked the other road
Smooth and easy to travel it showed.

I trudged on pondering when we'd meet,
Slow and steady I reached the summit,
Two hugging arms held me bound
With a victor's laurels I was crowned.

My friend who chose to slide down the slope
To enjoy the pleasures he did always hope
Lived in wild revelry and lost his wits,
Nobody could find his whereabouts.

I shall retell this with a deep sigh
Somewhere to someone before I die,
Two roads diverged in a yellow wood,
I took the one less traveled by.

My choice sure was heaven ordained,
For my spirit was glad to have obtained
The assurance of what I had sought
Would bring me more dividends than I thought.

Joe Anthony

154. To Be Led Than to Lead

Some people prefer to be led
Than to lead people forward,
Malleable and yielding their mind
They can be easily subdued.

They pick up crumbs on trail
Deliberately left by leaders,
But wouldn't lift a finger
To bake their daily bread.

They're like lengthening shadows
They have no identity,
Their life reflects indecision,
Their image is a mere farce.

Look at things through the lenses
Of hope and preferences,
The shadow of the Lord will fall
And night will turn bright day.

Joe Anthony

155. Reasons for Optimism

The world abounds in goodness and caring
People are sincere, always love declaring,
Ready to help out in times desolate
Attend even to the ignoble reprobate.

Love spreads its wings to shelter every person
No matter the origin, color, or religion,
It lingers even in the grieving bye-lanes
Its freshness enlivens and energy sustains.

Don't be stifled by polluted atmosphere
Look at the sky when it's blue and clear,
Why strain your eye through smog intense
Cherish the glimmer behind the scenes.

Marvel the glitter in the lingering tear drops,
Light a candle when darkness envelopes,
Give others space for the world's unlimited,
It's huge enough to shelter every dejected.

Treasure the laughter and smile of friends
Their singing and dancing in elation blends,
Care and concern in generous proportion
To bring about peace is a better option.

Gratitude, complements, empathy and trust
Can assist everyone to easily adjust,
Being punctual, loyal and thoughtful
Will make our endeavors truly successful.

Many are the wonders our world loves to hold
Need an eternity to count them as they unfold,
Why then should we waste time on evils?
Concentrate instead on the existing marvels.

Joe Anthony

156. Life Will Go On

Earth may quake, rains cause flood,
The sun won't stop to shine,
In violent emotion people spill blood,
But life's worth won't decline.

Dark clouds mar the face of the sky
But the stars won't be eclipsed,
Tears of sorrow blur the eye
Its hidden joy can't be stripped.

Rejection and support go hand in hand
Twin sides of the same coin,
Both are requisites to understand
How positivity to enjoin.

Despite all hardships, loss and pain,
Disputes, fallacy and spats,
Life will proceed and gloriously reign
Victorious in all combats.

Joe Anthony

157. With a Heavy Heart

My heart was heavily laden with sorrow
The blade of pain piercing my marrow,
Alone and weary like a weeping willow
I stood in anguish for reasons I didn't know.

Dark and foreboding clouds threatened my life,
Terror was alarming and suspense ran rife,
To confront the agents of conflict and strife
I needed the sharpness of a double-edged knife.

Engulfed in distress of failures and loss,
Unable cope with agonizing remorse
That choked my throat with its monster claws,
I held on firmly to the Savior's cross.

A shower of graces dropped from heaven
To combat this power insight was the weapon
I was expected to employ, I reckon,
Glad was the feeling for I'd learned my lesson.

Joe Anthony

158. Viewing a Blossom

I came to feel the fragrance
But the flower spoke out loud,
Bewitched by tone and elegance,
In awe and reverence I bowed.

Its voice was the cooing of a dove
Soft and melodious to the ear,
More like the whisper of love
Audible to those who're near.

Dignity, poise and grace
Smiled in awesome delight,
Portraying a virginal face
That was hidden from sight.

Its odor was pleasing and strong
Surging and spreading around,
Lingering eagerly to prolong
The viewing devotee spellbound.

My heart throbbed in elation
Couldn't suppress the feeling
Consume the essence, it's a potion,
An elixir to send me reeling.

Joe Anthony

159. Unhealthy Competition

My visions were effaced by the swipe of your rancor
And ambitions crushed with the hammer of hate,
My desires were boiled in the cauldron of your anger
Efforts of survival you crushed in envy irate.

Seething in fury at my success and fortune
Despite the realm of your wealth and power
Employed every method and means opportune
To thwart my ventures and my gains devour.

Success was the reward you had always sought
For all your attempts, illegal and wicked,
Too late you understood your mindset was rot,
Your empire and success had drooped and wilted.

Reason dawned on your stubborn opaque brain
Though delayed, your vision for revival glowed,
Acceptance of reality brought unenvious gain
Envy slithered away and our friendship was hallowed.

Joe Anthony

VIII

HUMAN GOODNESS

Human nature has a natural tendency to seek what is easy, pleasurable and satisfying. But deep within there is a great deal of goodness which is revealed in the way man responds to people and situations. More often these characteristics appear prominently on the surface and they compel us to look at man from a more humane and positive angle, instead of stressing on his negative traits.

160. Internal Strength

If you aim to conquer a mountain
You must scale first the peak within,
External ones are easy and simple
Once you have trounced the internal.

If at any cost you're determined to win
None can ever thwart your decision,
Road blocks emerge that often startle
But you'll succeed to skip every hurdle.

If you've decided to be a winner
Success and fame will with you linger,
When you aspire to ascend real high
Ensure to wear wings before you fly.

Let your life be an open book,
Record the essential, don't overlook,
It will reveal the struggles you faced
To overcome every ordeals unfazed.

Joe Anthony

161. A Gesture of Concern

Sitting by the window trying to propose
With my laptop a poem to compose,
What inspired me was a natural event,
I was overwhelmed by a chirping accent.

A little bird sitting on a clothesline
Tweeted a melody that didn't define
The nature of a songster in normal condition
For it differed in its song's rendition.

Hopping about in anxiety implied
That the basin of water it had espied
By an open window must have evoked
A worried response the scene invoked.

It perched on the brim of the container
Looked about and sensing no danger
Helped itself to a good bit of water,
Pecked at its body and ruffled a feather.

Chirped again, as if to say "thank you",
And left the scene so I didn't pursue,
The file on my laptop remained empty
So I recorded this enriching ditty.

When you offer a cup of cold water
To the least of the creatures of the Master.
Your reward is profound and also rare
That's the Lord's definitive gesture of care.

Joe Anthony

162. The Lady in White

She was young and beautiful,
Appeared slim and tall,
Her face reflected her innocence
Like flowers she diffused fragrance.

Radiant was her smile
Portraying a bewitching style,
Her breath had the essence
Of some angelic presence.

Her twinkling eyes were blue,
Had the power to subdue
Even the intimidating stalker,
Or a suspected imposter.

She walked on velvet foam,
With friends she loved to roam,
White was the dress she wore
Her rivals couldn't outscore.

Many craved for the privilege
To blend with her image,
Through green eyes some deemed
And rejected any praise she earned.

Success came to her with glory,
The elite knew her story,
Envied her pedestal position,
But refused to support her mission.

Bold and intrepid against odds
She could withstand their prods,
Emerge a winner noteworthy
And proceed with confidence her journey.

Joe Anthony

163. Humaneness

When problems and worries rise in alliance
And life's challenges meet with defiance,
Recall the trail of human misery,
Life wasn't ever comfortable or easy.

The heart of man is fashioned to remold
Opposing times and stages that unfold,
Transform obstacles to stepping stones
To success and satisfaction in all zones.

Heroism resides in the core of the heart,
In times of crises that emerges apart
Injects courage and hope to proceed,
Shields and uplifts the fallen to succeed.

Heroes emerge in every discipline,
Boost morale and stir us to action,
But the unsung heroes seeks no fame,
Selfless service is all they proclaim.

Joe Anthony

164. He Didn't Destroy the World

Why do you think the world isn't destroyed
Despite the wickedness, vice and fraud,
When it's flooded with all forms of evil,
And rule of villains and murderers prevail?

God could have annihilated his creation
A word was enough for this operation,
But in his wisdom, love and mercy
He weighed the goodness of the few as worthy.

Someone paid the medical expense
Of a poor woman who hadn't the finance,
Another picked up a wounded man
Reached him to a clinic in his personal van.

The school fee of the widow's boy was paid
From dismissal by the school he was saved,
With the help given to a destitute family
Everyone celebrated Christmas happily.

A consoling smile touched the girl's broken heart
Whose fiancés betrayal her life was torn apart,
From an orphanage a child was adopted
A home was provided though he was retarded.

The funeral expenses of a widow was met,
An expectant lady was offered a seat,
The bonus of faithful employees was doubled,
A loan was waived off the woman who struggled.

A begging child was glad of the coin,
From teasing an old beggar the boys refrain,
The freezing man was grateful for the cardigan
Put on him with love and compassion.

A free shave was given to a homeless man,
A meal shared with a classmate, an orphan,
The biker on duty was glad for the raincoat,
The jobless man found work and support.

A lift was offered a girl who was desperate
To attend an interview for she was late,
An umbrella sheltered a little child
Wet in her uniform, as helplessly she cried.

A tiny bird was rescued by a lame child,
Retrieved a drowning dog in filth defiled,
Trees were planted for fruits and shade,
Help came to clean up the shopping arcade.

God saw the goodness and was quite pleased
His decision reverted, his anger appeased,
He decided to give us yet another chance
And offered us ways our merit to enhance.

Joe Anthony

165. Disabled But Noble in Mind

Alone she lay by the open window
Paralyzed from an attack of polio
Watching life go by in unending flow,
And traffic like streams winding in a row.

She blesses all who by her hut strode,
Her humble dwelling next to the road
Where tourists halt by the waterfall
To refresh at her father's tea stall.

This opening isn't just a window for her
But a real friend with life and fervor,
In her loneliness she sees the world
And watches intently the beauty unfurled.

This window talks to her and often sings
When the wind enters and freshness brings,
Though immobile she rests on her pillow,
Travels the world through this window.

She spends her time in writing stories,
Poems and songs of joy and worries,
Hope and belief urging her to pursue
Her life of content, though it seems untrue.

She knows her supporters could offer her happiness
But they can't give her a window like this,
She won't leave it, even if she's obliged,
It is through pity her needs they provide.

She has never walked but she believes
She will one day when Jesus she meets,
Run about in heaven holding his hand
Make up for what was missed in this land.

She can't abandon the window that stood by
Revealed the meaning of life as it should be,
Unknown to the world quietly wish goodbye
Before she receives the blessing to die.

Joe Anthony

166. In the Purview of Parents

The greatest happiness that parents find
Is to have children with them aligned,
Give them the best of food that nourishes
Provide a warm home that ever flourishes.

It's good to see children growing up in virtues,
Observing and promoting family values,
Even after marriage living their own lives
And promote faithfully the family vibes.

We may go hungry but feed our children
Their failure and success are our concern,
Our burden and distress vanish in the bargain
This cherished profile will always remain.

To fathom this truth you need to be a parent
A father or a mother, it isn't different,
For everything to us was a lovely daughter,
Who filled our life with fun and laughter.

Without her we couldn't ever think of living
For we had watched every step of her growing
For her sake we decided that we should forgo
The gifts of more children to our home bestow.

That joy prevailed till she turned eighteen
When she eloped with a man we'd never seen,
I complained to the Lord but his reply shocked me:
"I was sending more but you didn't want any".

Parents are guilty of being possessive
But children's attitude to parents is passive
You were selfish to have only one daughter
So God has accused you of being a defaulter.

Joe Anthony

167. A Friend's Departure

He lays still in peaceful slumber
A serene smile gracing his face,
And the glimmer of contentment
Wraps him in a warm embrace
By an intimate and mystic entity,
Familiar, favored and admired.

His chest heaved in easy pace
As his breath swayed rhythmically,
Like the ripples made by the waves
In an ocean of clear blue waters
When fondly caressed by breeze,
He seemed immersed in sanctity.

In enchanting reverie most solemn
Exceedingly pleasurable and crucial
Enthrallingly sublime and serene
Sure enough, he appeared bathed
In some dazzling celestial light,
Reposing in tranquilly undisturbed.

Suddenly he sat up with a jerk,
Looked around piercing the haze,
Rubbed his eyes for clearer vision
But fell back clutching his chest
As a sharp blade of pain arose
Slicing his ageing heart asunder.

He moaned in duress like a hound
Struck by an arrow from a bow,
Submerged in an ocean of torments
And ravaged by a gripping pain.
Glared at me in wonder which meant:
'Who are you and why here?'

Then he closed his startled eyes,
Heaved some silent words in sighs,
I prayed a while but he was no more
Never to return, forever gone,
To the land in sleep he had dreamed
The land of peace and contentment.

Joe Anthony

168. Her Breath Had Fragrance

In gasps came her breath
Intermittent and hesitant,
But was ardent and vibrant
Its freshness had depth.

It's odor when exhaled
Was that of a blossom,
Everyone felt awesome,
Refreshed and hailed.

Gentle and soft the touch
As it caressed my face,
Its kiss on lips had grace,
The hug was warm, I vouch.

Her breath created an entity
That never existed before,
A spiritual one you'd adore,
'Cause it possessed dignity.

In each puff she'd blown
There was life divine,
Acts of creation benign,
As his majesty had shown.

Her breath was now faint
Gentle and serene in effect,
She showed everyone respect
Didn't make any complaint.

Her breath glowed in fame
The shine was sheer pleasure,
Darkness felt the pressure
So crouched away in shame.

Joe Anthony

169. Passion for Flowers

Passionate am I about flowers
My heart contains a basket full,
The angel finds them delightful,
With them the altar he showers.

This basket contains a variety
Big and small, mellow and bright,
Multi-colored, simple and white,
And fully blossomed to befit a deity.

Many diffuse celestial fragrance,
All are pretty, winsome, attractive,
Some are costly, others less expensive
But all are fresh and full of radiance.

With these flowers Mary is pleased,
Glides her gentle hand o'er them,
Blows their fragrance into His realm
Pleading to have his anger appeased.

All these blossoms bow in devotion
Their emanating perfumes sing
Hymns of praise and thanksgiving,
When placed on the altar as oblation.

Their rainbow colors glorify the King
Their variety proclaims his genius,
These are all flowers most precious
In love and gratitude to Him I bring.

Joe Anthony

170. What Moves Your Heart

Spontaneous acts of selfless devotion
Bestowed on some unfortunate person,
Moves the heart to extreme emotion
Of appreciation and even admiration.

Tears lingering at the edge of the eyes
Of a poor child in the street as it lies,
A little girl sharing her food with another
Though the quantity indeed is meager,

Picking up and hugging an orphan child,
Aiding an old woman as her guide,
Standing up against a notorious offender,
Passing a jacket to a shivering bystander,

Diving to save a drowning person
Regardless of the effect of this action,
Not sending parents to old age homes,
Attending to a child who aimlessly roams,

When held helplessly at the traffic light
Dropping a coin in the beggar's plate,
Letting an old man skip the queue,
At a tragic sight rushing to the rescue,

Numerous are the occasions and sights
That delightfully ignite our aching hearts,
Overwhelm us with varied emotions
And enrich our lives towards finer visions.

Joe Anthony

171. The Family, An Altar

A family is like an altar
Where sacrifices you offer,
The victims represent the tally
Of the members in the family.

Parents are extremely delighted
When their Children are united,
Prepared to join in worship
And avail God's friendship.

The little they offer is much,
Surrendering helps to enrich,
The lit candles and flowers
Represent the family members.

Parents submit their off-springs
And children, their parents as offerings,
As one family unified
In sacrifice it is sanctified.

Joe Anthony

172. Human Relationships

Human relationships undergo changes
From pleasant to offensive or vice versa,
It's evident in nature at various stages
From frantic activity to total inertia.

When rivers flow from different directions,
Bringing each with its special attribute,
Converge and create varied dimensions
Turbulence is the gift offered as tribute.

As time passes and water flows smooth
Leaving behind all sediments resulted,
Bonding will help to comfort and soothe
Stormy reactions initially confronted.

Friendship and enmity are the twin sides
Making the coin of human alliance,
Place them in the forge that heat provides
Mold them a fusion of trust and reliance.

Joe Anthony

173. Discernment

My friends and colleagues who inspire,
Spur me to noble visions aspire
I do admire.

People with concern for others are dear,
They spread in abundance trust and cheer
I want them near.

Honest and hard work brings people success,
Which in turns leads to wealth and progress
My joy I express.

Some are ambitious and eager to rise high,
But in stress and strain they give up and sigh
My question is why?

I consider those who are crafty and vain
For portraying an untrue façade of gain,
Much to my disdain.

Strangers eager to offer support
Are prepared to guide and even escort,
They bring comfort.

Contentment, peace and love in good measure
Offer a life of unending pleasure,
It's a treasure.

Joe Anthony

174. Life of a Man of God

A man of God lives alone
Without any intimate life,
For his life isn't his own
But for those in strife.

He may be offered assistance
To take care of his quarters,
But not share his preference
Or his personal matters.

His secrets and apprehension
Are not revealed to any friends,
But offered to God with affection
In whom his commitment ends.

Who will comfort and console
In his anguish and despair,
When doubts assail his soul
Who will offer him a prayer?

When physically weak he survives,
But mental trauma is painful,
From prayer his healing derives
So he's immensely grateful.

The life of a man of God,
Is good from a layman's view,
But he cannot afford
Any pleasurable aims to pursue.

He does his personal chores
When free from priestly duty,
A life of comfort he ignores
To nourish the inner beauty.

At night he falls prostrate
Before the tabernacle to adore,
In the day, Mass he celebrates
And God's blessings he implores.

He became a priest for others
Not for a life of leisure
For no sacrifices he bothers
As suffering is love's treasure.

Joe Anthony

175. For a Reason

I am struggling here below,
It's only a short span,
My life's entire flow
Is to carry out his plan.

The road I daily traverse,
In the day and at night,
Turned on me perverse,
Didn't relieve my plight

I found stranded at the gate,
The entrance door was shut,
I pondered over my fate
Of my labor's result.

A faithful slave I worked,
Haven't had much rest,
Never my duty I shirked
Still felt utterly bereft.

Will I ever enter that door
That I still see shut,
Must I be left on the shore
Devoid of a rowing boat?

I shall never surrender
To any evil intent,
With trust I shall render
To the Redeemer my consent.

Joe Anthony

176. Love Regained

Expressive eyes with tears brimming,
Soft as a whisper her voice quivering,
Barely audible with emotions underlying,
Weaved by threads of her past Intertwining.

Her life was a tapestry of sorrow and pain
Made up by warps and wefts of strain
That evoked memories of past torment,
A period of ongoing rebellious ferment.

Her revelation struck a lightning bolt,
Churned his stomach and strangled his throat,
He listened spellbound unable to react
Swayed unsteadily under its impact.

She weaved a spell he couldn't escape,
Love was rekindling and taking new shape,
A swirl of unresolved feelings emerged,
A torrent of emotions flooded and surged.

As time elapsed a brighter space dawned
They were drawn closer forming a new bond,
Their love blossomed like a rose in spring,
Fragrance and happiness had an upswing.

Love is a mighty force that can move mountains
An agent that transforms and balance maintains
An antidote for every malady we face
A legacy of hope and trust to embrace.

Joe Anthony

177. Overseer

I perched on a lonely massive boulder,
Squatting poised in the middle of waters,
Like a royal eagle to every beholder
Surveying how life's optimism falters.

Tongues are lapping up water avidly
Savoring the taste of floating matters,
Confronting the onslaught of ships fiercely
Levelling wavy folds to avert disasters.

Zooming in motion of demonic extent
To capture a fleeting prize awarded,
Risking life with pride and contempt
Drown together with their kindred.

Colossal ships overshadow tiny yachts
Like pride looming over gentle humility
Power and submission are extreme slots
Yet they coexist in ample cordiality.

Bellow, hoot, boom, like thunder in the sky
The squawking of seagulls pitch in between
Everyone is distressed by this cacophony
Yet many will relish it with interest keen.

Violent motions propose to compromise
As day flows into the ocean of night,
Placid and serene, the waves harmonize
To transform the scene to a pleasing sight.

Joe Anthony

178. Praying for Others

Praying for others is a merciful deed,
People we don't know too feel its need,
And their conditions affect our lives
Our emotions too vibe with theirs.

People often ask us for our prayer
Seeking God's help when in despair,
There's no guarantee to affect a cure
But to offer our prayers we can assure.

They consider us to be agents of grace
Hope that God our entreaty will embrace
Offer comfort and cure and rewards galore
Alter their condition and health restore.

Man is not pious or holy by nature
Only an unworthy sinful creature,
But his trust could decide His reply
And whatever offer He might supply.

Joe Anthony

179. In My Winter Days

When the last bird leaves me alone
And the chill of winter creeps through my bone
My snow-wrapped leaves wither away and die
Exposing my anguish to the mist enveloped sky.

Lonely, engulfed in the yawn of oblivion,
Choked by the frozen clutch of the season,
And pelted by elements fierce and cruel,
I stand a skeleton in torments utter brutal.

Animals or birds don't seek my shade,
Butterflies and honeybees appear afraid,
Birds have left their nests desolate,
My situation is precariously delicate.

Afraid of courage and divested of beauty
I stand like a phantom evading my duty,
At such occasions you never fail to appear
To sustain my life and sprinkle good cheer.

Joe Anthony

IX

DAILY LIFE EXPERIENCES

Life is replete with experiences. Some are more expressive and impacting than others. Pain and sorrow, death and loss, distress and exultation, hope and despair, the list never ends. We go through such situations all our life but if we are able to bail ourselves out and traverse a sane and redeeming path that has been revealed in our quest, we have climbed our Everest.

180. Monsoon

Monsoon's the season of purging and freshness
Of what is sordid and wilting in uneasiness,
Cast by the spell of the fairy of the season
Who glides gently in blithesome abandon,
Swaying her wand to transform the earth
To effect a mutation, suggesting a rebirth.

She sends her lightning to zigzag the sky,
To hide the twinkling dots lets the clouds fly,
She blows her storms in a mighty fury,
With leveled lances of rain in wild hurry,
Her thunderous voice rips the heaven asunder,
And creation echoes in awesome wonder.

Nothing can withstand her ravaging onslaught,
Destruction and torture seem her birthright,
Floods devastate and deform landscape
Its beauty and glory from ruin can't escape,
All forms of life and project get stranded
Can get back to order if time is granted.

Once the spell is done, nature takes over,
Calms every nerve and allays every fear,
Infuses passion to get back to normal
Considers what occurred as most natural,
Decks with beauty every hill and meadow,
Restores the lost glory by displaying a rainbow.

Joe Anthony

181. Why Joy, Not Sorrow

We are allured by joy and happiness,
Is sadness and sorrow impulses revolting?
If joy and sorrow are sweet bitterness
Why burst out laughing than burst out crying?

We keep aloof from themes of sadness
Unprepared to accept harrowing truths,
Stars appear bright in total darkness
As sorrow can better heal our wounds.

In sadness we learn to grow and mature,
Drink from his chalice, you'll know for sure,
Pain's a catalyst to creativity ensure,
So too in pain your vision is secure.

Joy and pain your interior transform,
Pain urges you to stand up and perform,
Exit your comfort zone, to duty conform,
For sadness is richer than joyless reform.

Joe Anthony

182. A Make Over

My heart was a desert of dejection
With sand dunes of arid desolation,
Not a blade of grass dared to invest
Such landscapes they abhor and detest.

Every scrap of life emerged sordid
Leaving all my emotions morbid,
My mind was a burning cauldron
Generating steam of lethal passion.

The oasis of grace didn't endorse
Shady palm trees tried to enforce,
Nor its insipid, stagnant wetness
Slaked my thirst for true existence.

Then of a sudden, out of the blue,
A healthy seed of remorse grew,
Popped its head above the sod,
An inner awakening soon followed.

A desire for true repentance emerged,
My interior barren land in grace resurged
Flowers of delight bloomed fresh again
This ambience helped me heaven attain.

Joe Anthony

183. Our Legacy

This is the feather of a bird
Whose name I've never heard,
Nor have I seen it before
So I decided it to ignore.

But its texture and color
Were not normal, but subtler,
Intrigued to a great extent
To probe I gave my assent.

I don't know if I did right
A female one to call it,
It could have been a male
For it left no trail.

It wasn't a familiar face
Must be of a distant race,
But we know it came here
Seeking something familiar.

Whatever was its object
In the precious item it sought,
We shall never come to know
But glad such exists so.

We don't know its name
Nor where it came from,
But it lighted a spark
And left behind its mark.

The bird left us its feather
As a token of its pleasure,
What's the core of our legacy
That we're leaving for posterity?

Joe Anthony

184. My Receptionist

You are at the reception
All dressed up in glamour,
Did anyone offer suggestion
How to retain your demeanor?
Uttered a kindly word,
And praised your attitude,
Status you preferred,
Or your aptitude?

Has anyone expressed
Your presence they enjoyed?
Were your clients impressed
By the way you toiled?
Did you smile at the person,
Who stammered as he spoke?
Who trembled with exertion,
Tried his weakness to cloak?

Did anyone utter a "thank you"
For a favor you offered?
The nasty toddler did you pursue
Who with your things fidgeted?
The old woman seemed hostile,
Were your nerves on fire?
Her toothless friend though docile,
Had nothing to inspire.

Did you truly represent
The vision of your employer?
Tried your best to prevent
Every harm through a lawyer?
Was your day well spent
To leave a trail of joy,
Or a wound of discontent
In those you seemed to annoy?

Were you truly genuine
Always in your career?
Then enjoy a sleep divine
With conscience pure and clear.
As into slumber you plunge
Does your conscience say
Your flaws you must expunge
To earn you another day?

Joe Anthony

185. Unproductive

Desperate attempts are on the way
To bridge the gap of loss and delay,
Only bubbles appear on the foam
Nothing substantial seems to perform.

Things are arid, sterile and bleak,
Trees portray a bony physique,
Plants bear no flowers despite good feeds,
If flowers appear they bear no seeds.

Devoid of stamina, divested of urge
All elements are in need of a purge,
People and animals soaked in sloth
Fail to provide any effective growth.

A rebirth of courage and the need to prosper,
The desire to live a life more proper,
With effort empowered by undiluted goal
Can transform and bring it under control.

Joe Anthony

186. A Funeral

The evening was cloudy
Rain was suspended
It wasn't ready.
When it relented
It was a deluge,
Mighty and huge!

The rain subsided,
The funeral entry,
Slow and subdued,
Into the cemetery
Was slow and solemn
In one single column.

The father kissed
His son's forehead,
The mother placed
Her face on his head:
"Son don't worry
We're not sorry.

"We know you're bound
To heaven's abode,
Our wishes abound
And on you are bestowed,
We'll meet you there
Your joy to share.

Joe Anthony

187. Lessons from Animals

If animals could themselves ever assert
They'd have sued us for cruel assault
Every case filed in a court of law
Could've send us to prison for our flaw.

When we refer to creatures as low grade
Calling them cats or dogs we degrade,
Heaping insults on innocent animals
And consider them as mere mammals.

They are not only our faithful friends
To guard and protect us are their ends,
Always appear at our beck and call
In affectionate manner before us crawl.

Animals are loyal, sincere and friendly,
Many are kept as pets and treated gently
Their genial manners delight everyone,
To the young and old they are good fun.

They are genuine, do not shame them,
They observe nature's laws then why condemn?
Don't attack each other, except for food,
For their devotion salute them we should.

Joe Anthony

188. Opposites Must Exist

Love and surrender never divorce,
So do silence and tumult,
Joy and pain are in alliance
As do shadow and light.

We feel warm in the winter's cold,
In happiness emerges tears,
Toil and sweat always blend,
In white, blackness appears.

Work and wages are partners,
Defeat to victory is docile,
To death resurrection matters,
Hatred and love must reconcile.

Death and birth are like twins,
Union over separation grins,
Heaven over damnation wins,
But coexist as God wills.

Joe Anthony

189. The Sky

Sometimes it's a vast and appalling void
Naught is visible even to a strained eye,
Scary gigantic shadows are displayed
Concealing the significance they imply.

Often it's a blossom of glittering stars
Clasped by leaves of colorful fleece,
Its fragrance is perceived only by bards
Whose mind is receptive and in peace.

Tucked beneath is a bundle of shades
Of varied designs of unearthly glow,
Unthinkable is the beauty that pervades
Only an artist's inner eye would know.

Joe Anthony

190. Higher Education

We need to be furnished with some high degree
To apply for a decent and well-paying post,
So we struggle through courses that guarantee
A Degree in hand of which we can boast.

Well armed with degrees, the best of its kind,
We turn in for interviews in reputed concerns,
Patiently queue up, the wait we don't mind,
Hate to hear the same disgusting response:

"We'll get back after the committee decides,
Inform you when to complete the formalities,"
And you think your fortune with life coincides
But sadly that call won't relate to realities.

Still you linger on, depressed, yet hoping,
Time moves on laden feet yet patiently you wait
Expecting the call for which you had been longing
Until you realize there'll never be an update.

How long to wait, your patience erodes,
Disheartened you divert your quest to other fields
For any kind of jobs your mind readily enrolls
And gladly accept the result your pursuit yields.

You're prepared to do even jobs menial
For you've realized every task has dignity,
Your mind is receptive, your attitude genial
So you accept the offer without hostility.

Your morale uplifted, your mind submissive,
You take the odd job and are satisfied,
You dismissed every post that was lucrative,
In this fulfilling job you took much pride.

Friends may query why such lowly jobs
For a man of dignity with a high degree,
You shirk your shoulder but your heart throbs
For a better contract in future you foresee.

Joe Anthony

191. Invest Well

Emptiness is a vacuum
Lonely like a tomb,
Discard, it's futile,
Makes you a servile.

Submerged in despair
In pursuit beware,
Skeleton feigns shape,
Prevents your escape.

When chasm looms
Emits toxic fumes,
Why waste labor
For a trifling cipher?

With conscience clean
And your vision keen
View things with caution,
Enjoy a life of fruition.

Joe Anthony

192. Suffer the Consequences

Diseases are varied and innumerable in kind,
Many suffer terminal and in bed are confined,
Others are contagious and are quarantined,
Some affect our body, others our mind.

Many have remedies for permanent cure,
Availability of some medicines is still unsure,
Research for new ones is under debate,
All are awaiting an urgent update.

Heaven had been sending us persons astute
Who could have contributed in this pursuit,
But we killed them in their mothers› wombs
Cruelly tore apart their heads and limbs.

We hear of pigs eating their new born,
To which animal man who kills the unborn
Be compared to for his inhumanity
For man has become his greatest enemy.

Many of the aborted could have been doctors,
By our heinous crime we became monsters,
They could've been saints or agents highly gifted
And in our endeavor could have assisted.

The right to live isn't only for those outside
But also to those who in the womb reside,
The loss is ours for the crime of abortion
For we resisted the purpose of creation!

Joe Anthony

193. The Caged Parrot

The parrot's out of the cage,
Struts aimlessly about,
Wants in chat to engage
And with the dog interact.

Ventures into the pig sty,
Couldn't bear the stink,
Trots back home in a hurry
It is thirsty for a drink.

The wings had been clipped
When it was first brought,
But their growth now started
A chance to escape, no doubt.

Often I watch, in rage
Yells out different names,
Strides about the cage
And the caretaker it blames.

Hangs on a bar by the beak
Or dangles by its claws,
Often I hear it shriek
Appreciates every applause.

An amusing scene to view,
A pleasing song to hear,
This would have been true
In its natural atmosphere.

Unlock the door of the jail,
Give it freedom to fly
It'll explore the trail
After the final goodbye.

Joe Anthony

194. The Veil

The veil is a rather intriguing item
An appendage of a woman's attire
She could be a nun, a bride, or a Muslim,
It reveals or conceals the truth entire.

It disguises or hides the true nature
It leads us into a deeper insight
But also reveals its inner feature,
Into what's being covered from sight.

Behind the veil is an enigmatic reality
Something beautiful and quite mystical,
We can see the essence of vitality
Not fully revealed by the mere physical.

The veil symbolizes ownership in Islam
For women is the property of their men.
Once we realize that the veil isn't a sham
We can readily accept it then.

The veil signifies the consent of a woman
To the loving care of her faithful spouse,
Her trust and confidence in her chosen,
His Christ-like leadership will espouse.

As a loving partner and soul mate
She's been specifically consecrated
To steer that vessel to a safe ambit
And a sacred union consummated.

Catholic women often wear for modesty
A veil over their heads in deep reverence,
Wedding veils are symbolic of purity,
A bride's state of chastity, as evidence.

To lift the veil refers to the unraveling
Of ignorance and prejudice prevalent,
To expose the truth by unveiling
The obscure, this appendage is relevant.

Joe Anthony

195. Cremate or Bury

Rising expenses and ever shrinking space,
Burden and troubles of planning process,
Time constraints being an unending trial,
Shy away people from opting for burial.

Cremation is simpler and less expensive,
Disposing of body is not offensive,
It doesn't understate respect or regard,
Nor overlook the show of a decent façade.

Burial is a practice that shows deep reverence,
The most appropriate Christian response,
Burial of the body adds weight and dignity,
Heightens its sacredness and reflects nobility.

A funeral conducted with a burial service
The best way to mourn someone's demise,
Lowering a coffin deep emotions imply,
Most people deem it a formal goodbye.

The body isn't just a container for the soul
But the most Holy Spirit's receptacle,
God will resurrect and glorify the body
Fitting to respect and honor it holy.

There's no intrinsic dissent to cremation,
Though preference is for burial tradition,
Many factors can influence the decision,
Selecting the mode is a personal option.

Joe Anthony

196. Don't Fear Death

Death, your look with savage intent,
Your deceitful snares that entangle
And lethal fingers clenched to strangle
Scare me not, I view with contempt.

Brutal and barbaric in appearance
Ravenous as a beast of the wild
Exploding emotions all defiled
Shall not threaten my existence.

You have no hold on me at all
Save only what's allotted to you
So shift aside and obey curfew
Come when you hear my final call.

I won't waste my precious time
In morbid and futile pondering
My life isn't for squandering
It's God's gracious gift sublime.

Joe Anthony

197. Old Age Homes

Retirement homes are the basements
Where you dump the discarded
Away from botheration and harassments
By the vulnerable, ailing and aged.

Isolated from the family they'd built
Nourished, cared and loved always
In solitude and sorrow now are left
To grieve in their final earthly days.

Basic amenities, security and support
Are provided with an attitude casual
Hoping with inmates build good rapport
That is most often genuinely natural.

But shame and hurt by force being sent
To nursing home despite having their own
The unbearable stigma grandparents resent
Living in gloom, dejected and unknown.

Growing ***old*** can be fearful and bleak,
If children are selfish, harsh and uncaring
When their parents are aged and weak
Despite being brought up without suffering.

Many high earners with status and class
Can't put up with their clumsy ways
Leave them to fade, in obscurity pass
Through a desolate and agonizing phase!

Children must obey, love, even worship,
For parents stand for God in human form,
To be with them is the blessing to cherish
If they want with God's wish to conform.

Joe Anthony

198. The Ambulance

What's your reaction when you hear
The siren of an ambulance alarmingly near
In the thick of noonday traffic in race
And the driver restlessly maneuvers for space?

The patient could be in serious condition
Needing emergency supervision,
We can't gauge the depth of his pain
Nor judge if he will die or remain.

We can't enter the realm of his mind
To assess sensations of any kind,
The varied emotions that may intervene
Are in general similar at every scene.

He could be a person of ripe old age,
Or an unfortunate victim of human rage,
A fatal accident of any kind,
The chances are many and undefined.

We would sympathize with the impaired
And with the family and friends who cared,
Offer a prayer to the Lord for a favor
To send a speedy remedy to recover.

Joe Anthony

199. Our Fulcrum

When laid down by stress and strain
And find no source to remedy the pain,
We seem to let things go out of hand
In dismay entertain a bleak façade.

We can move mountains of glaciers,
Subdue all hurdles and cross barriers
Of negativity, failure or even despair
Using the fulcrum of faith in prayer.

Faith can launch us into trust intense
Build a formidable wall of defense
Against all hindrance most obdurate,
And help us our sufferings to tolerate.

The wall will collapse before our eyes
Our firm, unflinching faith never dies,
It will work wonders to perform our task
And proceed to our eternal stop to disembark.

Joe Anthony

X

CHILL OUT WITH JESUS

Companionship is an innate desire in every normal human being, to be with another person, to spend time together. It's one of the reasons people get married or seek out like-minded friends. We also seek the company of beings of a spiritual dimension, like saints, angels, and even God himself. Many good people enjoy this spiritual union. The following poems reveal man's urge to be in the company of God and experience his love and mercy.

200. The Kiss That Blistered

You approached me with an evil mind
Concealing the actual truth behind,
Employed a gesture most divine
To betray me, and my name malign.

Your repulsive kiss burnt my face,
Blistered the skin, leaving a trace
Deep within my mind and heart,
I can't tell you how I felt hurt.

There wasn't remorse for your move,
Lingered not for pardon or reprove,
Chose the gallows in desperate hurry,
Stifled your conscience to avoid worry.

How I waited for you to return
Filled with remorse and contrition,
My heart was heavy with concern,
Ready to bless and offer you pardon.

You'd been with me three long years
Managed well our financial affairs
Heard my words and witnessed my deeds
Their effect didn't alter your needs.

Your bad example lures the gullible
To fall victim to actions fallible
End up with you in total surrender
Unaware you're a heinous offender.

Joe Anthony

201. Let His Will Prevail

At the table of silence and solitude
Assailed by urges I ponder and brood,
Resisting onslaughts of ungodly images,
And a colony of unbridled messages.

My mind wanders over the precipice
Of unattainable demands for relevance,
Waves of dissipation and of despair
Seethe through me, it's beyond repair.

Old regrets are brutally reopened,
I'm helpless, my sorrow has deepened,
The sores in my mind are truly hurting,
I am a bundle in the arms of suffering.

My chalice is full, even to the brim.
There's no other way but to trust him,
Who calmed the sea and stopped the gale,
I pray humbly that his will prevail.

With healing arms he embalms my wounds
And wraps me up, his mercy abounds,
With his breath he dries my tears,
Calms my nerves and allays my fears.

Highly overwhelmed by His grace,
I let a hurricane of glory and praise
Explode from my heart and arise
To magnify him without compromise.

Joe Anthony

202. Blissful and Free

At the foot of the cross I was sitting
Pondering over Jesus' suffering
Assessing how he achieved his mission
And the way he bore His passion.

The open wound close to his heart
Implied an urge for love to impart,
From my eyes hot tears emerged
At the eyelid's edge they lingered.

I felt drawn to share his vibe
And pined for his sadness imbibe,
Suddenly a teardrop fell on my chest,
Made a scar, my welcome guest.

Heaven was sharing my pain entire,
I dabbed the wound with the balm of desire,
The rhythm of this eternal thirst
Throbbed ardently within my breast.

This scar wrapped me in snug embrace,
Its soothing kiss had the fullness of grace,
I immersed myself in the waves of longing
And soared into the realm of its origin.

I entered the eye that shed the tear
And found my eternal lodging here,
Though still at the foot of the tree
My fervent spirit was blissful and free.

Joe Anthony

203. Thank You Lord

My heart with gratitude overflows wild,
In torrents the deluge gushes unbridled,
For all the miracles you have performed
I don't know how to put across my word.

There are no terms to express what I feel,
There are only emotions that cannot reveal
Until they explode under intense pressure
To be felt and experienced in full measure.

It's your mercy that brought me thus far,
Given me life and healed every scar
That I may remain in the state of grace
Be united with you to sing your praise.

On the sacred paten I place my body
And in the chalice let my blood embody,
Lay your sacred hands on this sinner,
Transform and sanctify me a winner.

My body and blood after consecration
Become our body and blood for oblation,
When your body on my tongue melts
It permeates all over and within me dwells.

In your presence for all sins I atone,
The void is deep to survive alone,
Your mercy overrides your love for justice,
Thus you offer me a heavenly hospice.

Thank you also for the crosses you send,
Willingly accept them and Calvary ascend
Deeming this a privilege to share in your pain
And offer them to the Father in expiation.

In reparation and penance for my violations
Grant me forgiveness for my transgressions,
Send me death when I am fully prepared,
So, worthy and blames I shall be declared.

Joe Anthony

204. My Deal with Jesus

Lord, let's make a fair deal
Between the two of us,
Take me you definitely will,
For time don't make a fuss.

I've no problem in coming,
Take me only from the chapel,
When I am prostrate adoring
Imbibing mysteries you unravel.

This is my ardent desire
For death this place you assign,
Into your bosom I'll retire
Direct from this holy shrine.

We've talked it over before
You didn't affirm or deny,
Many a time I did implore
There was no definite reply.

Let's make things more clear:
It won't be when I drive,
Nor in anguish or fear,
Nor to sleep I strive.

You took home your saints
With Mary by your side
Let me die in her arms
And Joseph be my guide.

My life is yours for good
As it has always been,
Every rupture I withstood
No space exists between.

Yours was the face I beheld
When reason on me dawned,
Yours shall it still be upheld
Our union in intimate bond.

Joe Anthony

205. Your Strange Ways

You caress me with pain
Embrace me with sorrow,
Over my wounds in vain
Some sealant dust you throw.

My mind is plunged in agony,
My heart can feel the torture,
My ego is floating in misery,
In anguish I see no future.

You took away from me
The crutch on which I rely,
My inner eyes can't see
In your absence I cry.

My vision is partially blurred,
My senses are benumbed,
My life's meaning you erased,
To frustration I succumbed.

You fill me with longing
But keeps my heart empty,
My prayers you keep ignoring,
It can't be your offer of plenty.

Yet in this distress and hurt
The proof of your love is concealed
Through the experience of discomfort
Your love and compassion is revealed.

Joe Anthony

206. Intimate Talk

Prayer is being one with God.
What you do or think or say
Can be the ideal way to pray
And adore the Divine Lord.

Prayer is the primary axis
On which life should revolve.
The orbit I shouldn't miss
From which I must evolve.

Prayer is the root of existence,
The gentle breeze that unveils
God's concealed countenance,
To plead his will ever prevails.

Prayer penetrates every fence,
Can soften a hardened heart,
Or fortify a crumbling defense,
And hope and trust sure impart.

Prayer is Jacob's ladder
That bridges man with his God,
With humble and honest candor
Can ascend on his own accord.

Empty all pain and grief,
Struggles, failures and flaws,
Extent your hands for relief,
You won't miss His applause.

Joe Anthony

207. God Loves Children

The Lord surveys the earth for souls
Prefers the delicate, young and pure,
Empowers them with crucial roles
To guide all elders for heaven secure.

He firmly demands that they be brought
Before his august presence frequently,
To receive his blessings and to be taught
To love, obey and sere him faithfully.

Children are angels before the Lord
Whose authentic image they truly portray
He showers them with worthy reward
And protects them from going astray.

Guiltless, trusting and honest by nature
They reflect virtues of devotion and care,
His joyful company they love to treasure
And abundant happiness with him share.

They are like candles flickering and melting
Like flowers diffusing fragrance and wilting
Decking his altar in profound reverence,
Living their life according to his preference.

Joe Anthony

208. The Altar of the Cross

Sit before the Sacred Host
For veneration exposed,
The Lamb of God, the victim,
Sacrificed for his kingdom!

The cross was the altar he sought
To offer his life for our fault
Now he's enthroned on the altar
So we sing hymns from the Psalter.

He hears what you whisper,
He knows the cause of your whimper,
You may prefer to be silent,
His concern for you is vibrant.

For him words are redundant
Impartial is his judgment,
Your posture defines your ego
That's enough for him to know.

Joe Anthony

209. In Praise of Mary

Mary my loving virgin and mother,
Into your hands in total surrender
All that I am and possess I offer
To be your faithful child forever.

You've been my best helper and friend
On whom I have been blessed to depend,
You never fail my needs to attend
But is ever there from evil defend.

All joys and sorrows with equal pleasure
I do accept and cherish as treasure,
You offer gifts without a measure,
They help me live in comfort and leisure.

Daughter of Father, Spouse of the Spirit,
Who conferred on you the needed merit
To bear God's son after Gabriel's visit
Your joy was blissful beyond limit.

From an remote and unknown nation
You were made the queen of creation,
Your submission brought us liberation,
From your son we obtained salvation.

You are considered King David's tower,
Enthroned beside your son in power,
The Almighty's precious and peerless flower
Lavishly disperse your fragrant odor.

Always a mother yet ever a virgin,
In your little womb you held the Son
Whom the whole world couldn't contain,
In your life we've found our origin.

Joe Anthony

210. Fear Not

Been in a storm, did panic intrude?
God's in control, all will be subdued,
Discern vigilantly what he provides,
Clearly visible and nothing's in disguise.

Look at the world in smile and cheer,
Retain details of every venture,
Meet Him frequently and apprise Him
The gains secured with vigor and vim.

The beast within might unshackle
The chain of virtues gained in battle,
The lukewarm souls could sink in peril
To withstand its onslaught it won't be able.

Raise your heart and spirit to the Savior,
Hold on to the string of grace in prayer,
Fear not for He will draw you up
Into that celestial realm of His love.

Joe Anthony

211. The New Bethlehem

A cave where animals found shelter
You decided to make it your home,
Its unhealthy state you didn't alter
Diffused the cave with your shalom.

You brought status and recognition,
Your presence changed this place,
Gave it a superior dimension,
Made it a heavenly space.

A new Bethlehem is within me
Make worthy this cave unholy,
The inn's loss was the shelter's gain,
By avoiding sin we blessings obtain.

Reborn into this pristine manger
With the Lord in the altar's chamber
A sublime privilege so gracious
Offered me a treasure most precious.

I'll wrap you with warmth and love,
My whisper as the cooing of a dove,
I will sing you a lullaby divine
And in your cuddle I will recline.

Let this manger stay lifelong
Beg our childhood you prolong
In worship your mercy we implore
With the Magi and shepherds adore.

Joe Anthony

212. My Awesome God

Let your mercy, Lord, shine through my sins,
Like the rays of the sun in all its brilliance
Penetrate the depth of my nurtured weakness
Unclamp your right arm and hug me with meekness.

Your love far exceeds the love of all saints
Who accepted martyrdom without complaints,
I want my love for you profound and intense
And erupt in spasms violent and immense.

When I abandoned and from you departed
In guilt and shame I felt broken-hearted,
The fragrance of your generous forgiveness
Embalmed my wounds that throbbed in harshness.

No more neglected, forsaken or forlorn
Your love has weaved me a wreath to adorn
My unworthy head as a token of grace
Which I gratefully and lovingly embrace.

Joe Anthony

213. He Made Me Eternal

Deep in the mire I was alive
Gasping for breath to survive,
Struggling desperately to surface
Having lost all life's purpose.

Hope appeared just a dream
I sank deeper in despair extreme,
A sudden splash, I felt a shudder,
A cross slipped from his shoulder.

His hand was gentle and firm
He pulled me up with his arm
The mire was no more in the marsh
He had leveled it by the splash.

He left the ninety nine to seek
The lost and wandering sheep
By a transformation internal
He made me forever eternal.

Joe Anthony

214. Hold on to the Cross

Hold on firmly to the cross of Christ
Whenever you are assailed by doubt,
The only thing that matters after all
Is the truth you'll never falter or fall.

Things we prioritized in life and sought
Has become a distant afterthought,
Things we own become insignificant
If the cross isn't deemed magnificent.

People look at everything but not at the cross
They would prefer to see beauty and gloss,
Your belief in the cross you must enforce
And boast in the cross and shout in applause.

The world watches you and your goodness
But hesitant to accept you as a witness
Hardened sinners dare not confront
The Gospel message that's direct and blunt.

If you think you're holy and deserve heaven
And heaven isn't heaven, unless you're therein,
You're like the Pharisee with his righteousness,
Unlike the publican who exposed his abjectness.

Hold on to the cross when death's at the door
Request like a child your worth to restore,
A child that boasts in the cross of Christ
Can remain innocent all day and night.

God has made an appointment for each
One that enables us for death to beseech,
When our chance comes we can discern
How we can boast in the cross in turn.

Joe Anthony

215. In His Company

I sit before your picture
Reading the Sacred Scripture,
Your look brings me delight
Your eyes are alive and bright.

The whisper of your breath
Sweeps over me with warmth,
My joy I cannot contain
For it's beyond the mundane.

The mystical touch of your fingers
Has a soothing effect that lingers,
Your mercy hugs me with fragrance
In awe I stand in your presence.

Immersed in your embrace
I obtain the needed grace
To reply to the query of the poser
The right solution and the answer.

Prodigal are you with gifts
To receive everyone persists,
It's wise to you we surrender
And live with you in splendor

Joe Anthony

216. Be with the Host

Every child is the reflection
Of God's eternal projection,
His finger extends beyond death
Our inheritance is our wealth.

If you're at God's right hand
The world's at your command,
The devil you can confront
Your life won't bear the brunt.

Of every joy you can boast
If you're in tune with the host,
The gift of life you're offered
Is a boundless treasure conferred!

Joe Anthony

217. A Humble Expectation

"If only I could touch
The hem of his garment",
Was the awaited wish,
For a fulfilment.

It was an excellent thought,
Simple was the desire,
Needed no effort
But worthy to inspire.

An effort was the demand
Stretch out a little far,
For help was near at hand
In concealed assent by her.

She hadn't made a request
But a reason-skipped feeling,
Yet her wish received permit,
The touch brought her healing.

Joe Anthony

218. God's Holiness

Attaining holiness is not an option
In the divine strategy it's a decision,
We can harness the Lord's holiness
To transform and upgrade our lowliness.

God demands his consuming fire
Should engulf us and mold every desire,
Without destroying he makes us immortal,
And welcomes us at his sublime portal.

God had set the standard so lofty,
None can reach it, for we are faulty,
It was a recipe for despair and fear
So he had to come down to help us adhere.

Sin is a spiritual suicide before God
When in sin, we're nothing but fraud
God is closer than we to our own selves
His olive branch beckons us to where he dwells.

Joe Anthony

219. All Alone

I need your support
For heavy is the weight,
Can't bear the burden
I'm a weak person.

Betrayed and broken,
Tormented, downtrodden,
Tears fall in torrents,
Woes my vision portents.

The cold touch of death
Seems to choke my breath,
Revive and offer me succor
Be my protector and Savior.

Joe Anthony

220. The Temple of God

Extreme was his anger
Like a blazing fire,
When the house of prayer
Was made a trade center.

Bargaining and arguing
And dishonest dealing,
They traded their goods
From the temple courts.

He grabbed a long cord,
Took a step forward,
Made a strong whip
Their businesses to flip.

He drove out every animal
Both sheep and cattle,
Overturned the tables,
Scattered their shekels.

Severe was the warning
For his temple defiling,
And making a sacred space
Into a haggling place

This makes us aware
Our body to declare
A temple of the Spirit,
With reverence to treat.

Restore its purity,
Its pristine beauty,
Dedicated for worship
And adore his Lordship.

Joe Anthony

221. If Jesus is Lost

If Jesus is lost, everything is lost,
You're a wreck, you don't exist,
Your edifice crumbles into dust,
Your life is profaned by distrust.

Wriggling in the womb of somber void
Fear and despair you fail to avoid,
Your dreams and goals have lost track
Vague is your vision, a total setback.

Search and you'll find was his injunction
For life without him is not an option,
Life is bestowed in generous portion
Jesus will raise his hand in benediction.

Joe Anthony

222. Let Down Your Net

We struggled all night casting our nets
That caught only distress and regrets
Though we ventured away from the shore
We failed and returned our effort to deplore.

"Let down your net into the deep,
A large enclosure let it sweep,
These are unchartered territories
That could reveal rare mysteries".

A repaired and redeemed net is cast
Into an ocean serene and vast,
The time was ideal for a good catch
Though we knew of a possible mismatch.

The net was pulled towards the boat
Filled with bubbling life afloat
In shock and awe the neighbors helped
The catch was the most unexpected.

Joe Anthony

223. The True Bread

Like a dew drop that alights gently
And spreads on a tender leaf evenly
The sacred host descends and rests
Silently on my tongue and melts.

It permeates my entire essence
Transforms me anew by its presence,
Day and night it stays within me
Never leaves me to mourn in agony.

I feel our heartbeats synchronize,
His whisper seeks me to divinize,
The odor of his breath weaves around
I inhale its freshness pure and profound.

Joe Anthony

224. Waiting for the Call

Like warm waves of water
Ebbing away in soft whisper,
Like the cool mist in winter
Sieving through green pasture,
My breath is gently gliding,
For the pearly gate it's aiming.

Silver streaks sparse yet long
Privileged to my head belong,
Ruffle a mellow farewell song
In unending cadence prolong,
Wanting to keep me company
Till I embrace my destiny.

My journey is a little delayed
Extend my hour of sunset I prayed,
Felt it wasn't yet time to fade
Leaving my debt to God unpaid,
Having settled my account now
For the final call I bend and bow.

Joe Anthony

www.ingramcontent.com/pod-product-compliance
Lightning Source LLC
LaVergne TN
LVHW041013150826
845672LV00001B/76